# INTRODUCTION

Experts predict unprecedented intergenerational asset transfers within the coming decades – $20 trillion in the next 20 years alone. Chances are, some of that money will be yours, transferred either during your lifetime or at your death. In other words, whether you live to be 70, 80 or even 90, you are likely to have assets that outlive you – "excess" wealth that will be transferred from you to others. What you choose to do with that excess – now and then – is what this book is all about.

Our focus, in question and answer format, is on three essentials of wealth transfer:

- Communicating with family members and advisors;
- Creating a plan that reflects your goals and values; and
- Protecting your wealth from unnecessary taxes.

At current estate tax rates, no one can afford *not* to think about transfer taxes.

*Part One* (chapters one through three) begins by considering some hard questions, from "What is a good wealth transfer plan?" to "How should I involve my family in the planning process?" to "Which assets should I discuss with my estate planning attorney?"

In *Part Two* (chapters four, five and six), we cover the fundamentals of wealth transfer planning with clear explanations in layman's terms.

*Part Three* (chapters seven and eight) is about fulfilling your objectives through tried-and-true strategies that are built on open communication with your family and advisors. We emphasize the importance of lifetime gifting, both as a way of "test-driving" your plan and as an effective tax-saving technique.

Look to *Part Four* (chapters nine through eleven) for a discussion of special assets – from the company retirement plan to the family business. You should finish this section with a real sense of what the wealth transfer planning process can do for you.

*Part Five* (chapters twelve through fifteen) provides an in-depth conversation about transferring wealth to the next generation and to charity. Be ready to examine the broad range of techniques that our clients have used to create their legacy.

And finally, *Part Six* provides direction and assistance for using the information presented in *Legacy* to begin preparing your own wealth transfer plan. Throughout, we talk about how to integrate your financial objectives with your values, thoughts and beliefs to create a plan that you understand and that gives you comfort – both now and in the future.

# PART ONE

# GETTING STARTED

# CHAPTER ONE

# Understanding Wealth Transfer

*In most undertakings, the first step is often the most difficult – wealth transfer planning is no different. You may not think you need a wealth transfer plan because you are not married . . . or have not retired . . . or are not wealthy. This chapter dispels common misconceptions about wealth transfer planning and encourages you to create a plan that reflects your personal values as well as your financial objectives.*

### 1. *What is wealth transfer?*

Ideally, wealth transfer is a lifelong process of allocating your wealth to provide for and protect the people you love. If you are charitably inclined, it is also an opportunity to benefit the broader community and establish a tradition of giving.

One component of wealth transfer is providing for transfers at death, commonly referred to as "estate planning." Another equally important component is transfers during your life, or lifetime gifting. Lifetime gifting yields tax advantages while allowing you to see the effects of your planning and, sometimes, to reevaluate and reconsider.

A good wealth transfer plan begins with your ideas, your knowledge and your intent. This book is designed to help you make the strategic journey from these first thoughts to a plan that is truly your own. Along the way, it is helpful to keep in mind that there is no perfect combination of wealth transfer strategies. Instead, there are many alternate means to achieve your goals.

Despite important differences, we do find that every effective wealth transfer plan has these things in common:

- It takes into account current realities, both emotional and financial.

- It succeeds in meeting well-defined objectives.

- It represents the collaborative effort of a team of professional advisors.

## 2. *Who should have a wealth transfer plan?*

You should have a wealth transfer plan if you want to ensure that your wealth is distributed according to your wishes in a tax-efficient manner. If you have minor children, aging parents, a spouse or anyone else who relies on you, a comprehensive wealth transfer plan is even more critical.

One misconception about estate planning is that it is only for the wealthy or the old. This is untrue. Younger people also have obligations, become incapacitated or die. Even if you have no family – or are just starting out – you will still want to leave your assets to specific recipients.

In sum, a wealth transfer plan is important for *every* adult.

## 3. *When should I create a wealth transfer plan?*

The sooner a plan is put into place, the greater protection for family members who would otherwise be forced to make choices for you without your input. Timely planning and implementation give your objectives a head start and allow for their full evolution.

SITUATION: FAILURE TO PLAN.

Rob and Yvonne are in their 40s, with four school-age children. Rob has just inherited $2 million from his parents and both spouses are doing well professionally.

The couple has thought about doing some "estate planning," but has never been able to agree on who should serve as guardian for the children – Rob's brother or Yvonne's sister. Besides, they think of themselves as too young to worry about death or disability.

One evening in November, the couple is involved in a traffic accident. Rob is killed instantly; Yvonne lingers on for four months before passing away.

After a year of bitter litigation, Yvonne's parents, who are in their 60s, gain custody of the children, who are still unsettled by the chaos following their parents' death. Yvonne's father, who is not a sophisticated investor, loses what is left of the children's inheritance.

As time goes on, the family experiences a chronic shortage of funds, exacerbated by the health problems of the aging guardians.

SOLUTION

With a basic wealth transfer plan, Yvonne and Rob could have:

- Executed wills designating a guardian for their children;
- Established a trust with a professional trustee to manage the children's inheritance; and
- Executed powers of attorney and health care directives to enable family members to act for them in the event of their disability.

They never imagined just how damaging the consequences of their inaction would be.

### 4. How can I create my wealth transfer plan if the tax law is constantly changing?

Your attorney will know how to craft a plan that is flexible but at the same time consistent with current law. Tax law is fluid by nature, changing constantly as new social and fiscal policies emerge. The estate tax law is no exception – there have been several major revisions since its enactment in 1916.

Future changes in law will probably require future adjustments of your plan. The alternative – to wait until the law changes "once and for all" – is unrealistic. Dying without a plan – or with a plan that does not reflect current law – can be very costly.

### 5. What basic questions should I consider when creating my wealth transfer plan?

Like so much in life, your wealth transfer plan will only be successful if you've carefully considered your goals and objectives. For example:

- What do you want to accomplish with your money?
- How do you want your wealth to shape your family's future?
- What legacy do you desire for future generations and for your community?

Once you clearly understand your primary objectives, your advisors can show you how to achieve them, strategically and tactically. As you work with them, consider:

- Who should receive your assets? How much of your wealth should you leave to your spouse, children and grandchildren? To other relatives? To charity?

- Which assets should they receive? You can easily divide your cash and investment portfolio, but how do you divide the family business or the vacation home? Which assets do you want transferred to specific recipients?

- When and how should you transfer wealth? Should you make some gifts during your lifetime when your beneficiaries might need your gift more, and you can see the impact? Or, should you make all transfers at death under your will and revocable trust? Should you transfer wealth outright? In a trust? As a family partnership interest?

- What are your plan's foreseeable outcomes? Look ahead and anticipate how your gift will impact your beneficiaries. Will it cause family conflict? Is it the safest way to gift? Is it the most tax-efficient way? Every plan has consequences – personal, family, business, tax, legal and financial.

### 6. I am concerned about maintaining my current lifestyle in retirement. How do I decide how much to leave others?

Generally, you should consider gifting only after concluding that you have sufficient assets to sustain your own lifestyle. Once you are confident that you have adequate funds to cover your needs, you can begin thinking about gifts to your family members, friends or charity. Your finan-

> In determining your retirement needs, don't forget to consider inflation as well as your spouse's future financial security.

cial advisor can help you determine your cash flow needs and sources.

### 7. How should I divide my wealth among all of the potential beneficiaries?

For many people, the first concern is their spouse, then their children, then their grandchildren. Once they decide how much is enough for one group, they move on to other recipients.

In many situations, the simple answer – "leave everything to the children equally" – may also be the most sensible. Families with significant wealth however, typically consider a broader number of prospective beneficiaries. For example, they may use a dynasty trust to provide for multiple family generations. In addition, they may expand their circle of potential beneficiaries to include their extended family, non-family members as well as charity.

One way to start the planning process is to list everyone – family, friends and charity – who is truly important to you. Considering all potential recipients ensures that your plan fully reflects your circumstances and goals. At this point, don't worry about

> **A FAMILY MISSION STATEMENT CAN BE CREATED TO:**
>
> - Help families determine what their core objectives are, reflecting their expressed values and beliefs regarding wealth – its creation, use, preservation and distribution;
>
> - Guide decision-making by the family members and their advisors around the use of wealth; and
>
> - Provide the foundation on which a wealth transfer plan is designed, leading to the maximum use of resources for family members and society during their lifetimes and in future generations.

mechanics: your estate planning professionals will have many ideas on how to structure your transfers into a coherent plan.

## 8. *How often should my wealth transfer plan be updated?*

You should update your wealth transfer plan whenever you experience a significant life event that is likely to affect how you want your wealth transferred.

Recognize, too, that the focus of your wealth transfer plan will evolve over time. For example, when you are a young parent your primary concern is likely caring for your children, allocating enough money to raise them in your absence and selecting the right guardian to serve in the event of your incapacity or death. In contrast, as you grow older, your children may be self-sufficient, your grandchildren may be beginning their careers and families, and you may have a new partner. You may also be caring for elderly parents, supporting them financially and emotionally. With each event or life stage come new ideas, concerns and opportunities that should prompt you to ask yourself "Does my plan reflect my goals?" If your answer is "no," speak to your advisors and make the revisions that are needed to bring your plan into alignment with your

WHEN TO REVIEW YOUR WEALTH TRANSFER PLAN

- "Life" event
  - Death of spouse or child
  - Serious illness
  - Birth of a child or grandchild
  - Employment change
  - Marriage or divorce
  - Sale of business
- Move to a new state
- Change in asset value or composition
- Change in your health
- Change in your goals and objectives

new objectives. At a minimum your plan should be reviewed every three to five years to incorporate changes in applicable state and federal law.

### 9. Does creating a wealth transfer plan take a lot of time and money?

A good wealth transfer plan is well worth the investment. While you will need to hire skilled professionals to develop, implement, manage and administer your wealth transfer plan, these expenses are necessary. Proper planning can reduce the taxes you pay – and may save you or your beneficiaries future court costs and attorney fees.

If you want to *save money*, however, you'll need to *spend time*. The more time you invest in locating relevant documents and putting your wishes in writing, the less preparatory work your advisors will have to do. This should go a long way toward reducing the final cost of your plan.

Ultimately, you need to remember the purpose of wealth transfer planning – to ensure your property goes to the people you want promptly, efficiently and with a minimum of confusion and red tape.

# CHAPTER TWO

# Engaging Your Family Members and Advisors

*Studies show that wealthy households – defined in our research as those with investable assets over $1 million – are increasingly seeking advice when it comes to tax planning and wealth transfer planning. Simultaneously, there is a growing trend toward more open communication within families about values and money. This chapter sets the stage for meaningful dialogue with family members and for productive discussions with your advisors.*

### 1. How should I involve my family in the wealth transfer process?

Open communication with family members, professional advisors and charitable beneficiaries is essential and integral to wealth transfer planning. While only you can determine how much to communicate and with whom, an open discussion gives families an opportunity to come together and address important issues, perhaps for the first time. These discussions can minimize subsequent misunderstandings.

> Some families organize a family meeting to discuss wealth transfer issues. Those taking this route find that the structure of a planned meeting can help facilitate meaningful dialogue among and between generations and can set boundaries and objectives for the discussion.

Communication helps you avoid basing your plan on faulty assumptions. For example, if you are planning to have friends or family members as your trustees, executors or guardians, consult them about their willingness to serve in this capacity. These jobs are not easy, and not everyone will accept the responsibility. If they agree to act on your behalf, you will want to talk candidly about your expectations and objectives to reduce any uncertainty over their role.

### 2. How can I better prepare my children to handle their inheritance?

Money management skills should begin as soon as your child understands the concept of money. Starting with a small allowance, teach your child about budgeting and prioritizing expenditures and about deciding how much to spend, save, invest and donate.

A critical part of the learning process involves setting financial limits, in other words, learning to say "no." For many families, regardless of wealth, this becomes a balancing act – attempting to provide what your child *needs* without giving her everything she *wants*.

Parents who want their children to have good financial skills instill financial discipline, creating self-sufficiency. They involve their children in their own business and financial decisions. Using these strategies, they give their children financial skills and strong financial values.

> **THE BASIC SKILLS EVERY CHILD NEEDS TO MASTER BY THE AGE OF 18 ***
>
> 1. How to save
> 2. How to keep track of money
> 3. How to get paid what you're worth
> 4. How to spend wisely
> 5. How to talk about money
> 6. How to live on a budget
> 7. How to invest
> 8. How to exercise an entrepreneurial spirit
> 9. How to handle credit
> 10. How to use money to change the world
>
> *From "Raising Financially Fit Kids," by Joline Godfrey.

### 3. *When is the right time to talk to my children about our wealth and their inheritance?*

Discussions with your children about the value of money and the responsibilities that accompany wealth should begin when they are young. Try to develop a lifelong dialogue that will help them mature financially. As time goes on, you'll be able to refine your wealth transfer plan and feel confident that your children will be able to handle – emotionally and financially – whatever wealth you choose to transfer to them.

At appropriate ages, children should have some idea about their inheritance, as well as when and how they will receive it. This way, they can better plan their own financial future.

### 4. Should I discuss my plans for charity with my children?

Philanthropy is more enthusiastically accepted by children when they are involved in the process. One strategy is to involve your children in this aspect of your wealth transfer plan – as board members of a private foundation, for example, or as donor advisors of a donor advised fund.

### 5. How common are sibling conflicts over inheritances?

Sibling conflict over inheritances is all too common. As with so many of the issues we've discussed, open communication is your best strategy. If one child's inheritance differs from another's, make sure both children understand why.

> **CONSIDER AN "ETHICAL WILL"**
>
> The ethical will, also known as the spiritual will, is gaining in popularity. Unlike a traditional will that addresses financial assets, ethical wills deal with values, beliefs and ideals.
>
> Ethical wills are not legally binding, but they do provide an opportunity to offer comfort, love and forgiveness. Some choose to share them with loved ones during life, usually at an important anniversary or milestone event. Formats vary – from short letters to audio recordings to elaborate films.

### 6. What should I do if I plan to disinherit a child?

Think carefully about the effects of a potential lawsuit on other family members and on your wealth transfer plan as a whole. A disinherited child is very likely to challenge your will or trust in court.

If at all possible, discuss your plans with your child – she may not realize the depth of your feelings, and in some cases, honest discussion will lead to reconciliation. At a minimum, she will know not to count on a future inheritance when making her own financial plans.

7.  **What wealth transfer strategies work best in blended families?**

A variety of strategies will work as long as there is full disclosure to all those involved and the same standards are applied to each child. Given the emotionally charged atmosphere of some blended families, solid communication is key.

Typically, the thorniest issues arise when you and your spouse's finances, or those of your parents, are unequal. Many find that attempts to "equalize" inheritances in these situations are impractical and only lead to unnecessary complexity.

8.  **You referred to advisors with whom I should consult. Can you be more specific?**

Typically, your team of advisors will bring different expertise and diverse experience to the table; close coordination and collaboration among your team members are essential. The players should include the following (and might include others as well):

*Estate planning attorney*
To ensure you receive the benefit of up-to-date strategies, your attorney should specialize in wealth transfer planning. Don't expect a general practitioner or business lawyer to provide the expertise required by complex and significant wealth.

### Accountant

Good tax planning requires an understanding of your anticipated financial future. Your accountant is in an ideal position to evaluate potential strategies from the perspective of reducing your income tax burden. Be sure to obtain the services of a Certified Public Accountant, one who has passed the American Institute of Certified Public Accountants (AICPA) examination.

### Financial planner

A financial planner or consultant is responsible for creating a comprehensive financial plan and may also monitor its implementation. Financial planners can be professionally licensed by the SEC, NASD or state insurance commissioners. In addition, they often hold one or more professional certifications – Certified Financial Planner (CFP), Chartered Financial Consultant (ChFC) or Chartered Financial Analyst (CFA).

### Insurance professional

A knowledgeable insurance professional, one holding a Chartered Life Underwriter (CLU) designation, can assist your team in finding the most cost-effective ways to use insurance to meet your protection, liquidity and wealth transfer needs.

### Trustee, Executor and Guardian

If your wealth transfer plan includes trusts, you will need to name a trustee(s) who will be responsible for administering them according to their terms. Serving as trustee can involve years of effort, coordination with lawyers and accountants and detailed record keeping. Depending on the circumstances, a trustee may be a family member (including you), friend, professional advisor (attorney or accountant) or an institution (a bank with trust powers or other authorized trust company). If you use a trust and name an individual as trustee, you should appoint a successor trustee to serve if that individual, for whatever reason, cannot. You will also need to select someone to administer the disposition of assets not held in trust – an executor or personal representative. And if you have minor or disabled children, you will need to name a guardian.

### 9. *How do I find the right professional team?*

Chances are you are already working with a trusted financial advisor – an attorney, accountant, financial planner or private banker. You can begin your search by asking any of these individuals for a referral. They will most likely provide you with several names and may suggest you meet with each for an initial interview. The interview process will help you make an informed decision.

A second approach, contacting a professional organization, can also work well. For example, if you need an estate planning attorney, lists of specialists within each state are available online from the American College of Trust and Estate Counsel (ACTEC) at *www.actec.org*. Or, you can contact your local bar association. If you need an accountant, you might consider the American Institute of Certified Public Accountants (AICPA). Many states also have local accounting organizations such as the Illinois CPA Society and the Florida Institute of CPAs.

## 10. *What should I look for when selecting members of my wealth transfer team?*

You want trained, experienced professionals who will work closely with you and one another to analyze your specific situation and recommend what is best for you and your family. At the same time, they must be people with whom you can share confidences as easily as you can discuss legal or tax issues.

Don't be afraid to ask questions:

- How much experience does the professional have with the issues that matter most to you?
- What is his professional training and accreditation?
- Are there any complaints registered with the licensing authorities?
- To what professional groups does he belong?
- What is his general reputation in the community?

Fees are important, but unless a quoted fee is clearly out-of-line, your choice of a professional should not be dictated by cost alone.

The most difficult part of the entire planning process may be finding the right people to help put it all together. Take your time at this stage. Hopefully, you and your loved ones will be dealing with your team for years to come.

### 11. *What information should I have ready before I meet with my wealth transfer team?*

Committing to thorough information-gathering is critical – careful preparation can avoid creating a plan based on faulty assumptions. And as we indicated earlier, advance preparation may help you reduce fees and other expenses in the long term.

Your advisors can provide you with a list of what information they will need from you (see Appendix A for a representative list). Equally important, your planning team needs to know your goals as well as any commitments you have already made regarding disposition of your assets – for example, to the daughter who works in the family business, the son who uses the family vacation home or the granddaughter who plays your piano when she comes to visit.

# CHAPTER THREE

# Understanding What You Own

*It is important not only to understand what you own, but also how you own it. Whether you own property individually, jointly or in some other form can significantly affect what your beneficiaries ultimately receive. This chapter discusses the various types of property you may own – highlighting some assets you may have overlooked – and describes the various forms of ownership.*

## 1. Which assets should I take into account when creating my wealth transfer plan?

In today's environment, assets may be scattered across the globe, subject to the laws and taxes of many jurisdictions. Your estate planner needs to know about everything you own – from second (and third) homes to investment properties and partnership interests. Your written inventory will serve as a valuable resource throughout the planning process.

## 2. I know there are many ways to own or title property. What are the most common and how do they affect wealth transfer?

Every asset – from investments to the family business – may be owned or titled in a variety of ways. How you choose to title each asset often affects to whom it will pass. Titling can also affect income and estate taxes, the procedures necessary to transfer the asset to the beneficiary and whether the asset will be protected from creditor claims. For all these reasons, your wealth transfer team will need accurate information about how your assets are titled.

**WHAT TO INCLUDE IN YOUR INVENTORY**

- Investment portfolios
- Annuities
- Homes, both primary and vacation, as well as time-share
- Employee stock options
- Interests in trusts and investment partnerships
- Insurance policies
- Retirement plans
- Business interests
- Real estate and mineral interests
- Outstanding notes and loans
- Intellectual property
- Collections

Assets with title documents clearly designate the record owner. Real estate, investments, bank accounts, vehicles and other personal property have deeds, certificates or bills of sale that document ownership.

You may own property in your name only or have a co-ownership interest with others as tenants-in-common or as joint tenants with rights of survivorship. In about half the states, married couples may hold at least some property as tenants-by-the-entirety. In situations where community property laws apply, married couples may hold separate property (usually property owned prior to marriage, or received as gifts or by inheritance) or community property.

Assets can also be owned indirectly. Examples include assets titled to a trust, corporation, limited liability company or limited partnership of which you are a beneficiary, shareholder, member or limited partner. Under certain circumstances, your rights to an asset may be time-limited. For example, a life estate gives you a right to enjoy property during your lifetime without the right to control its disposition at your death. Alternately, you may hold a future interest in property, such as a remainder interest in a trust. Each of these interests may be either vested or contingent. Vested interests are unconditional; contingent interests are conditioned upon the occurrence of a future event.

Your advisors can help you accurately identify your current ownership rights. The next step is helping you understand the alternatives and assisting you in re-titling assets, if necessary, to best meet your planning objectives (see pages 35 – 36 for a more complete discussion of ownership alternatives).

### 3. *Does a different set of ownership rules govern community property? If so, what are these rules and under what circumstances will I be affected by them?*

The majority of states use common law to determine property ownership. This means that the name on the account, title or deed determines the owner. On the other hand, nine states – Arizona, California, Idaho, Louisiana, Nevada, New Mexico, Texas, Washington and Wisconsin – have a special form of ownership reserved for married couples, known as community property. In simple terms, these states define community property as property acquired while people are married and domiciled in the state.

Though the applicable law varies somewhat among the community property states, in general:

- Each spouse can retain as separate property assets acquired before the marriage, or received during the marriage as a gift or bequest. Usually, earnings from separate property, including interest and dividends, are also considered separate property if they are not commingled.

- Property acquired during the marriage is generally considered community property owned one half by each spouse. Investments, real estate or other assets acquired by either spouse with his or her earnings during the marriage are generally community property.

When one spouse dies, his or her half of the community property passes as directed by his wealth transfer plan, or if there is no plan, according to the state's intestacy rules. The other half of the community property remains the property of the surviving spouse. The separate assets of the spouses pass according to their wealth transfer plans, or if there are none, according to state law.

Community property generally retains its character even if a married couple relocates from a community property state to a non-community property state. Therefore, it is important to alert your advisors if you are married and have acquired assets while residing in a community property state. Your advisor can determine the relevant state law and can also help you preserve the character of your separate property.

## COMMON OWNERSHIP ALTERNATIVES

### Individual
Owning property in your own name may not be the wisest choice. In the event of incapacity, personally owned assets are subject to guardianship proceedings if you do not have a durable power of attorney. Titling assets in your name may also increase your liability.

### Tenants-in-common
When two or more parties own property together as tenants-in-common, each tenant (co-owner) owns an undivided interest in that property. This means each owner can sell, mortgage, bequeath or dispose of his interest without the consent of co-owners. In other words, tenancy-in-common has no survivorship rights. And, if a beneficiary's objectives conflict with those of the surviving co-owners, it may be difficult to maximize the value of the asset. Creditors can reach property you hold as a tenant-in-common. In addition, tenancy-in-common expands each owner's liability: each co-owner is jointly and severally liable for the debts arising from the property.

## COMMON OWNERSHIP ALTERNATIVES *(continued)*

### Joint Tenancy with Rights of Survivorship (JTWROS)
With JTWROS ownership, your interest will pass automatically to the surviving joint owner. This means you cannot dispose of the asset under your will or living trust, even if you attempt to do so. The rights of survivorship take precedence. Title documents should clearly specify whether an asset is jointly owned as JTWROS or as tenants-in-common. Any asset – except IRAs, qualified retirement plans and insurance – can be jointly owned.

### Tenancy-by-the-entirety
Tenancy-by-the-entirety is available in about half the states and may apply only to certain types of property. It is a hybrid of joint tenancy that is reserved for married couples and provides extra creditor protection for marital property.

As with JTWROS, the surviving tenant-by-the-entirety automatically takes title to the entire property. In addition, there is protection against claims by a creditor of a deceased spouse: in the case of non-joint debts of a husband and wife, the property may not be partitioned, sold or encumbered without the permission of the survivior. Creditors common to both spouses can, however, claim the property. For example, a home held as tenants-by-the-entirety may be reached by the couple's joint creditors. Further, neither spouse may convey his or her half-interest without the consent of the other.

### Community property
In nine states, property acquired by couples during marriage is generally treated as community property, with each spouse holding an undivided one-half interest in each asset.

**4. I am a beneficiary of a trust. What exactly do I own and could it be included in my estate?**

A beneficiary of a trust can have a "present interest" – a current right to income and/or principal. Alternately (or in addition) a beneficiary may have a "future interest" – a right to receive income or principal or both – at some later date.

Determining whether a beneficial interest is subject to estate tax at death requires a review of the underlying trust document as well as knowledge of trust law, and of applicable state and federal tax law. Bottom line: These are complex issues that require the attention of a competent estate planning attorney.

**5. Are there any special considerations with regard to the ownership of life insurance?**

If you own a life insurance policy on your life, the proceeds will be included in your taxable estate when you die. One alternative is to have another individual or entity as the policy owner, for example:

- Your spouse;
- Your child;
- A business;
- An irrevocable life insurance trust (ILIT);
- A family limited partnership (FLP); or
- A limited liability company (LLC).

To choose the best form of ownership, consider the purpose of the insurance. Is it to replace income, to provide liquidity or to transfer more wealth to your heirs? Next, work with your advisors to determine the advantages and disadvantages of each potential alternative. A few basic considerations are described below.

### Ownership by a family member

If the insurance policy is owned by a spouse, the proceeds may be subject to estate tax at your spouse's death if your spouse's estate exceeds the available estate tax exemption.

If the primary goal is to pass wealth to children, it may make sense to name a child as owner. If so, the proceeds will not be subject to estate or income tax on the parent's death. As the owner, however, a child can make himself the sole beneficiary. Such authority may be problematic if the child is not financially responsible.

### Ownership by an irrevocable life insurance trust (ILIT)

An ILIT is an irrevocable trust that holds an insurance policy on your life. In other words, the life insurance policy names the trust as owner and beneficiary. When properly structured, upon your death, benefits are transferred directly into the trust and are *not* included in your taxable estate. Therefore, an ILIT can greatly increase the amount beneficiaries receive.

As with other irrevocable trusts, an ILIT requires a written document, a trustee and beneficiaries. The ILIT trustee follows your directions, as set forth in the trust document, regarding payment of insurance premiums during your lifetime and payment of insurance proceeds to the trust beneficiaries upon your death.

6. *Beyond protecting your family, can life insurance provide other estate planning benefits?*

Yes. You can use insurance to pay estate taxes, provide estate liquidity or fund the purchase of a business interest. Insurance can also be used to replace assets that are unavailable because of other planning strategies. For example, you might gift assets to charity and substitute insurance with a comparable death benefit designated for family members. Typically, that insurance would be owned by a *wealth replacement trust* (i.e., an ILIT) to keep the death benefit free from estate taxation.

7. *How are partnership interests and closely held stock treated for estate tax purposes?*

Like your other assets, partnership interests and closely held stock are subject to estate tax, based on their fair market value on your date of death. Value is generally determined by a qualified appraiser using well-established valuation guidelines. Substantial closely held assets should be appraised during the planning process and reviewed by your wealth transfer team. Over- or undervaluing assets may have a significant impact on the outcome of your plan.

8. *Much of what I own is illiquid. Is this something I should be concerned about?*

Yes. Estate taxes are due nine months after the death of the property owner. Debts, costs of administration and other liabilities can be due even sooner. In addition, a spouse or child may need funds for living expenses. An estate that holds illiquid assets, (e.g., a collection, real estate or family business interests) may be forced to liquidate assets at substantially less than market value.

If liquidity is likely to be an issue in your estate, it should be a central item on the agenda of your wealth transfer team. Potential solutions include buy-sell agreements, life insurance and lifetime transfers.

**9. *I intend to make substantial loans to my children. How should they be addressed in my wealth transfer plan?***

Outstanding loans are an asset of your estate and will be subject to estate tax at your death, based on their value at that time. They should be included in the asset inventory you share with your wealth transfer team, with careful documentation of their terms.

Making a loan is complicated – emotionally and from a tax standpoint. Most important, becoming your child's creditor can be uncomfortable, putting stress on the parent-child relationship. From a tax standpoint, if there is not a reasonable expectation that the loan will be repaid, the IRS may recharacterize it as a gift, with you or your estate liable for unpaid gift tax. Worse yet, if interest on the loan is set at a below-market rate, you or your estate may owe income tax as well. Finally, an outstanding loan can complicate your wealth transfer plan, decreasing liquidity and – if the loan is uncollectible – creating resentment among your other beneficiaries. Before making a loan, consider making a gift instead.

# PART TWO

# WEALTH TRANSFER FUNDAMENTALS

# People, Processes and Paperwork

*There are three basic planning documents: the will, revocable trust and power of attorney. While most people would benefit from having all three, the truth of the matter is that many individuals do not even have a will, or do not have a will that is up-to-date. In a recent survey, nearly one in four wealthy individuals stated that their will was last updated five or more years ago. In Chapter Four, you'll learn about each of these documents, the purpose each serves and the professionals whose assistance you will need.*

## 1. What documents would normally be used in wealth transfer planning?

Your wealth transfer plan begins with you – and with two documents designed to protect you and your loved ones while you are alive – *the power of attorney for property* and *the health care power of attorney*. A durable power of attorney for property gives the attorney-in-fact (the person who holds that power) broad or narrow rights – as you choose – to deal with property held in your name when you are incapacitated. A health care power enables a trusted friend or loved one to speak to health care professionals on your behalf when you are unable to speak for yourself. (With the advent of federal privacy laws, family members may not have access to doctors without this document.) In some states, a health care power is also used to convey your wishes about life-sustaining treatment. Other states require a separate document, sometimes called a health care directive or living will, which serves as an express direction to your attending physicians about life support decisions.

After your death, your power of attorney for property ceases to be effective. At this point, your survivors will rely on your *will* and *revocable trust* to express your wishes about the disposition of your assets. There also may be *irrevocable trusts,* established during your lifetime or at your death, as well as retirement plans and insurance policies with their own *beneficiary designations.* If your survivors are familiar with these documents before your death, the transition will be much easier for them.

## 2. How can I ensure that my directions about organ donations, funeral and burial arrangements, and autopsy will be followed?

Detailed instructions about your final disposition will be a helpful guide to your family members. This can be best accomplished by a separate letter, given to a close family member or friend – or, in some states, through the health care power of attorney described above. Although instructions can also be included in your will or trust, as a practical matter, final decisions are often made before family members have access to these documents.

## 3. What is a will and what provisions are typically included in it?

A will is a document by which you transfer the assets you own individually upon your death. A will also names an executor or personal representative to administer your estate, as well as a guardian for your minor children.

> A will usually does not dispose of all your property. Property can also be passed by gift, contract, joint tenancy with right of survivorship, or beneficiary designation.

Wills can be complex – or fairly simple. However, most wills contain provisions to:

- Name one or more executors, as well as successor executors;

- Name a guardian (for minor children);

- Authorize the executor to pay the decedent's debts as well as taxes and the expenses of estate administration;

- Direct the transfer of specific assets or specific dollar amounts to designated individuals or charities ("specific bequests"); and

- Dispose of the remaining assets.

### 4. *I have a revocable trust. Is it necessary to have a will?*

The short answer is yes. You will need a will to nominate a guardian for your minor children and transfer assets that should have been titled in your revocable trust during your life, but for some reason were not. For example, you may have neglected to retitle your investment portfolio in the name of your trust.

Wills are often used in conjunction with revocable trusts, with assets flowing or "pouring over" from the will to the trust. If an asset, for example a piece of real estate, is not transferred to your trust, it will not be subject to the trust's provisions. A pour-over will can take care of this problem. It provides that any asset not titled in the trust's name (or otherwise disposed of), will be "poured-over," or transferred, to it at your death. The terms of the trust will then govern the asset's disposition. See Chapter Six for a more detailed discussion of trusts.

### 5. *What assets will not pass under a will?*

Some forms of ownership – such as joint tenancy with right of survivorship – contain their own transfer provisions. And some types of assets – such as retirement plans – can only be transferred by means of independent beneficiary designations. Property that will not pass under a will includes:

- Property titled in a revocable trust;

- Property titled in joint tenancy with right of survivorship (or as tenants-by-the-entirety);

- Retirement accounts, IRAs, Keoghs and pensions;

- Life insurance;

- Annuities;

- Pay-on-death bank accounts;

- Transfer-on-death brokerage accounts; and

- Assets under beneficiary deeds.

### 6. *What is probate?*

Probate is the court-administered process of transferring assets (also known as the "probate estate") that are owned in a person's individual name. In most states today, probate is efficient and inexpensive.

The probate process generally begins with the presentation of the will to the state court by the executor named in the document. After formal appointment by the court, the executor gathers the assets; inventories them; pays debts, expenses and taxes; and distributes the balance of the probate estate to the beneficiaries. If the will is a "pour-over" will, the probate assets will be distributed to the decedent's revocable trust.

Because the court record is open to the public, probate makes your will a public document. In addition, many states require the executor to publish a notice to creditors and potential heirs, disclosing the existence of the estate as well as the name and address of the executor or her attorney. The downside to the notice procedure is an additional loss of privacy; the upside is a shortening of the creditor claims period. Executors may elect to go through probate because, under the relevant state law, the period during which creditors can make claims is often shorter than the comparable period for revocable trusts.

### 7. In addition to handling probate, what are the executor's responsibilities?

The executor manages the estate's financial affairs. This means that if the estate includes a business, the executor must manage the business until the estate is settled. In addition, the executor resolves potentially challenging legal and family conflicts – and defends and prosecutes estate claims.

Complex responsibilities like these may be a heavy burden, even for a family member.

### 8. Should I have more than one executor?

Before appointing an executor, ask yourself: *Will this person have the time, the skills and the energy for the job?*

Many times, one or more individuals and a single institution will be named to serve together as co-executors. This alternative can allow trusted family members to participate in estate administration without being overwhelmed and can be particularly helpful when assets include a business or other substantial assets. Involvement of a neutral third party can help assure the impartiality that is the hallmark of good estate administration. In other situations, individuals name a spouse, child or other relative to serve as sole executor, with the authority to hire professional assistance as needed. If you name more than one executor, your document should include procedures to resolve any disagreements.

Your will should also name a successor executor in case the primary executor dies or is unable or unwilling to perform. If you fail to name a successor executor, the probate court will appoint one – and that individual might not be whom you would have chosen.

9. *What considerations are important when choosing a trustee?*

By creating a trust, you place your assets, your wishes and the welfare of your family in the hands of your designated trustee. A trustee's responsibilities typically include:

- Investing the trust assets;

- Administering the discretionary provisions of the trust;

- Distributing trust assets;

- Recordkeeping, accounting and reporting trust activities;

### INSTITUTIONAL TRUSTEES

If you decide to use an institutional trustee instead of an individual, or as successor to an individual, consider:

- Whether trust officers would be personally and philosophically compatible with your beneficiaries. How would they interact with the family? Do they instill confidence?

- The institution's breadth of services. Can it handle special assets such as a family business or real estate? Does it provide guardianship and estate administration services? What functions are performed in-house and what are outsourced?

- Experience in and commitment to the trust business. Ask how long it has been providing trust services and how large the team is that supports this function. Also assess the strength and depth of the team.

- The fees charged and the services provided.

- Transaction and investment reporting; and
- Tax preparation and filing.

A trustee can be a person or an institution. Some qualities to look for include:

- *Loyalty* – A loyal trustee will act in the sole interests of the beneficiaries and will not be swayed by self-interest in the interpretation of trust provisions or in the management and distribution of assets.

- *Impartiality* – An impartial trustee will treat each beneficiary in accordance with the terms of the document and will not take sides.

- *Investment expertise* – If you select someone with extensive investment experience and resources, it is more likely your assets will be appropriately managed and preserved for your beneficiaries.

- *Tax and accounting expertise* – Transaction and investment reporting as well as tax preparation and filing are important trustee duties. Your trustee must see that this detailed work is done in an accurate and timely manner.

- *Continuity* – A trust may continue for decades or extend over multiple generations. In this situation, an institution may be a better choice than a series of individuals.

Many trust creators name co-trustees. Often, a professional trustee is appointed co-trustee together with a family member or another individual. You should also consider successor trustees and criteria for removal and replacement of a trustee. Whatever your choices, your trustees should be people to whom you can confidently entrust your property, secure in the knowledge they will have good relationships with your beneficiaries.

### 10. *What considerations are important when choosing a guardian for minor or disabled children?*

Deciding who will raise your child in your absence is one of the toughest decisions you'll face as a parent. When deciding upon a guardian for your children, you will want to consider:

- Willingness to serve as guardian;
- Age, health and judgment;
- Ability to provide the love, attention and guidance your children need;
- Compatibility with your values;
- If your child is disabled, expertise in dealing with the disability; and
- Ability to handle your children's inheritance.

Given this broad combination of factors, it is no wonder that many couples struggle. What they are looking for is hard to find: someone who has the necessary parenting expertise, as well as the sophistication to manage significant financial assets. Sometimes, it is simply not possible to agree on a single individual or couple with the right combination of skills. Faced with this situation, parents may choose to select a trusted family member as guardian for the children and a corporate fiduciary as trustee for their assets.

# CHAPTER FIVE

# An Introduction to Transfer Taxes

*When you transfer assets, during your life or at your death, tax may be due. However, there are steps you can take to minimize the amount you'll owe. After reading this chapter, you'll have a basic understanding of how to use available tax exemptions, exclusions and deductions to decrease your tax liability – and increase the amount you leave to your family and to others.*

### 1. *What are transfer taxes?*

There are three transfer taxes – the *gift tax,* the *estate tax* and the *generation-skipping transfer tax,* which impose a tax on transfers of wealth made during life or at death. One or more of these taxes potentially applies to each of your planned wealth transfers. Minimizing transfer tax requires thoughtful input from your advisors before transfers are made. Skillful use of exemptions, exclusions and deductions can reduce your transfer tax bill while helping you achieve your wealth transfer goals.

### 2. *How much of my estate will be consumed by estate tax?*

Assuming you made no taxable gifts during your lifetime, here is a simple way to estimate your estate tax exposure: take the value of your estate, less any debts. Subtract any assets that will pass to charity. If you are married and your spouse is a U.S. citizen, subtract the assets you will pass to her, either outright or through a marital trust. This net number roughly approximates your taxable estate.

If your taxable estate is equal to or less than the estate tax exemption available at your death, no federal estate tax will be due. Conversely, if your taxable estate exceeds your available exemption, federal estate tax must be paid (see Appendix C for exemptions and tax rates).

### 3. *Does each state have estate taxes? Do the same rules apply in every state?*

In addition to the federal estate tax, many states impose their own estate or inheritance tax. Depending on the circumstances, state estate taxes can be onerous and require careful planning.

(In Washington State, for example, rates have been as high as 19% on estates in excess of $9 million.) Rates, exemption amounts and deductions vary from state to state, so expert counsel is a must. Even if you are a resident of a state which does not impose an estate tax (such as Arizona, California or Florida), you may be subject to state estate tax liability because of property owned in another jurisdiction.

For those with homes in more than one state, the first question may be the most important: which is your state of domicile? In simple terms, your "domicile" is your permanent home – the place where you intend to return after temporary absences. Though you may have more than one residence, you can have only one domicile at a time. Domicile is determined by a number of factors, including vehicle and voter registration, employment, club memberships, mailing address and actual time spent in the state.

A second question is equally important: do you own property in *more* than one state? If so, it is possible that your estate will be subject to tax in two or more states. Although tax credits may be available in your state to avoid double taxation, there is no substitute for expert tax planning. You may decide to sell, gift or move your out-of-state property before death to avoid future tax problems.

Finally, remember that state estate tax, if it applies, is imposed *in addition to* the federal estate tax. Although a deduction is allowed at the federal level for the amount of state tax paid, the underlying assets are subject to tax at both the federal and the state level.

### 4. Is it true that the estate tax is being eliminated?

Although the federal estate tax is scheduled for a one-year repeal on January 1, 2010, it is doubtful that repeal will become a reality. Until Congress acts, the best advice is to focus on current law. Fortunately, there are tools your advisors can use *today* to maximize your estate's value and minimize estate taxes. The challenge for professionals is to stay abreast of new developments. The challenge for you is to make certain that your wealth transfer plan is modified and updated so that it remains as efficient as possible.

| CURRENT LAW PROVIDES AN ESTATE TAX EXEMPTION OF: | |
| --- | --- |
| Year | Estate Tax Exemption |
| 2008 | $2 million |
| 2009 | $3.5 million |

### 5. What gifts trigger gift tax?

The gift tax, which is generally paid by the giver, is a tax on transfers made during life. The law provides many opportunities to minimize your gift tax burden however, such as the unlimited gift tax deductions for transfers to a spouse or to charity.

#### Unlimited gift tax deduction for transfer to a spouse

Transfers made to a spouse, whether outright or in a properly structured trust, qualify for the unlimited gift tax marital deduction. These gifts do not trigger gift tax (see Chapter Seven for a discussion of lifetime marital trusts).

#### Unlimited gift tax deduction for transfers to charity

Transfers made to a qualified charity, whether outright or in a properly structured trust, qualify for the unlimited gift tax charitable deduction (see Chapter Fifteen for an introduction to charitable trusts).

### Annual exclusion gifts

The annual gift tax exclusion is limited to a fixed dollar amount per recipient per year (e.g., $12,000 for 2008). Married couples can give combined annual gifts (e.g., up to $24,000 per recipient in 2008) to individuals without incurring a gift tax. Annual exclusion gifts may be made outright, to an account established under your state's version of the Uniform Transfers to Minors Act or to a carefully designed trust.

### The unlimited gift tax exclusion for direct payments of tuition and medical care

The lesser known of the exclusions is the unlimited exclusion for direct payment of medical and tuition expenses. Types of permitted payments include doctor bills, hospital bills, health insurance premiums, and elementary, secondary or college tuition. These payments can be made on behalf of a family member, a partner, a parent or a complete stranger. As long as payments are made directly to the service provider, there will be no gift tax consequence.

### The $1 million gift tax exemption equivalent amount

During your lifetime, you can give away a maximum of $1 million – in addition to your exclusion gifts – without paying the gift tax. The Internal Revenue Code gives this exemption to you as a credit against your potential gift tax liability.

Depending on the circumstances, a lifetime gift may be more appropriate – and more tax efficient – than a transfer at death. Once you make a gift, the gifted asset is no longer part of your taxable estate. Furthermore, any growth in the asset's value will not be taxable to you.

### 6. *When is the generation-skipping tax imposed?*

The generation-skipping transfer tax ("GST") applies to transfers that "skip a generation," whether made during life or at death. For example, a transfer "skips" if made to grandchildren or to a non-family member more than 37½ years younger than the transferor. Exemptions and exclusions are available under the GST for properly structured transfers (e.g., the GST has an exemption amount, $2 million in 2008).

### 7. *What is a <u>simple</u> way to avoid transfer taxes?*

As you've seen, there is an array of exemptions, exclusions and deductions available under the gift and generation-skipping taxes. Your advisors can help you develop a program of lifetime gifting that works for you. Most likely, your gifting program will include:

- Consistent use of the annual gift tax exclusion – which allows you to make tax-free transfers of cash or property to an unlimited number of people each year; and

- Use of the unlimited exclusion for direct payment of tuition and medical expenses (including payment of health insurance premiums).

If you have substantial wealth, ask your advisors about taxable lifetime transfers that use part or all of your available gift tax exemption. And if you are charitably inclined, consider a program of lifetime philanthropy.

**8.** *If my beneficiaries receive appreciated assets from my estate, who pays the capital gains tax?*

Lifetime gifts of appreciated property (such as stock or real estate) are especially effective: both the underlying property and all future appreciation on that property are removed from your estate. Your beneficiaries generally receive a "carry-over basis" in the gifted property, i.e., their basis in the property is generally the same as yours.

Under current law, any asset included in your estate at your death is given a new cost basis, generally equal to its fair market value as of the date of death. For appreciated assets, there is a "step-up" in basis at death. This means that your beneficiaries will generally not pay capital gains tax when they sell appreciated assets received from your estate – unless, of course, the asset grows in value *after* your death.

**Example:** Years ago, you bought some real estate in Wisconsin for $10,000. At your death, your beneficiary receives a distribution of the real estate, which is now worth $1 million, from your estate. Your beneficiary's tax cost in the real estate is $1 million. If she sells the real estate for $1 million, she will pay no capital gains tax. In contrast, if you had gifted the property prior to death, your beneficiary would have a "carry-over basis" and would have to pay capital gains tax on a $1 million sale.

Some special types of assets, such as retirement assets or earned income, do not get a step-up in basis at death. There is also no step-up in basis for assets transferred during life.

**9.** ***What can I learn about wealth transfer planning from the mistakes others have made?***

Don't sabotage your own plan. Remember to:

- Update your existing documents as well as beneficiary designations on retirement plans and life insurance;

- Implement your plan, e.g., fund your trusts and properly title assets;

- Consider lifetime gifting; and

- Analyze the impact of transfer taxes – before making significant transfers.

In the following chapters, we will discuss how you can accomplish your wealth transfer objectives in a tax-efficient manner.

# The Role of Trusts

*Trusts can help you achieve a wide variety of wealth management and wealth transfer objectives – with great flexibility. Their usefulness goes far beyond their ability to reduce taxes. Whether you want to maintain your current lifestyle in retirement or create a legacy for generations to come, trusts can help you achieve your financial and personal goals. Chapter Six introduces the most common ways in which trusts are used and provides practical information on how to create a trust.*

## 1. How does a trust work?

A trust is a flexible tool that can help you achieve a wide variety of wealth management and wealth transfer objectives. From a technical perspective, it is a legal relationship generally involving three parties:

- The *grantor* funds the trust and decides its terms. This includes naming beneficiary(ies) and establishing distribution standards, e.g., requiring distributions for a beneficiary's health and support.

- The *trustee* is an individual or institution, chosen by the grantor, who holds the legal title to trust property, pays taxes, manages assets and makes distributions to or for the benefit of the beneficiary. Often, the grantor will appoint co-trustees – a family member and a trusted advisor – to jointly manage the trust. This approach can work well if you need the sophisticated services a professional can provide, but feel a family member may better understand your situation.

- The *beneficiary* receives income and/or principal from the trust according to its terms.

Some trusts – such as a revocable trust – allow the same party to be the grantor, trustee and beneficiary. Other trusts however, require separate parties to take on these different roles.

## 2. *Why use a trust?*

Trusts can meet a wide variety of objectives. The most common are to:

- Safeguard the financial interest of loved ones;
- Reduce taxes (certain types of trusts only);
- Maximize the amount that will transfer to beneficiaries;
- Fund a charitable endeavor;
- Provide continuity of management within your lifetime and across generations; and
- Manage property during incapacity of the grantor or beneficiary.

## 3. *How do I know which type of trust will best meet my needs?*

Your advisors can determine which type of trust will meet your needs (see pages 66 – 67). Relevant factors include whether you:

- Are married (or have previously been married) and if it is your first or a subsequent marriage;
- Have young children or grandchildren;
- Want to safeguard your beneficiaries' inheritance from lawsuits, creditors or divorce;
- Have spendthrift or irresponsible children to protect; or
- Want to make a charitable gift.

*Revocable trusts*, often referred to as "*living trusts*" are the most popular.

### Revocable trusts

A revocable trust is simple to understand and use: you title your assets in trust name to use for your own benefit during your lifetime. In contrast to an *irrevocable trust,* which cannot be revoked or "undone," a revocable trust can be revoked or amended during your lifetime and permits withdrawals.

A revocable trust does not have an independent tax identity until you die. During your lifetime you personally pay taxes on the trust's income and capital gains. Typically, you remain trustee of your revocable trust until your death or incapacity, at which time a successor trustee whom you've also named, would administer the trust. Within the trust document, you designate the beneficiaries and the terms of distribution to those beneficiaries.

Of the potential benefits from a revocable trust, these four are most often cited:

1. *Protects privacy:* Unlike the terms of a will which become public during probate, the terms of a trust usually do not become part of a public record.

2. *Helps manage your affairs if you become incapacitated:*
   Your successor trustee will manage the trust if you become incompetent or ill – the alternative may be lengthy and expensive guardianship proceedings.

3. *Ease of asset administration:* Assets are identified and titled in a way that facilitates management.

4. *Useful for multi-state assets:* If you have real estate in many states, a revocable trust avoids *ancillary probate* for out-of-state assets.

In sum, a revocable trust is extremely flexible – you can add or remove assets, change investments, change beneficiaries or completely unwind the trust and re-title the assets back into your own name.

**4. *What benefits will a revocable living trust not provide?***

Although a revocable trust is an important wealth transfer tool, it *will not*:

- *Save taxes.* Unlike certain types of irrevocable trusts, a revocable trust is tax neutral. It doesn't save income or estate taxes. Trust property is treated as held by you for federal and state income and estate tax purposes. If the estate triggers federal or state estate or inheritance taxes, your executor must file the appropriate tax returns.

- *Negate the need for a will.* You still need a will to dispose of assets not owned by your trust and not otherwise disposed of. If you have minor children, you need a will to nominate their guardian.

- *Affect non-probate assets.* As with a will, a revocable living trust won't control the disposition of jointly owned property, life insurance, pension benefits, retirement plans or other assets payable to a specific beneficiary.

- *Protect your assets from creditors.* The grantor's creditors can claim assets held by a revocable living trust. In fact, since assets in a living trust cannot be probated, they could lose the protection of probate's statute of limitations, i.e., creditors may have a longer time period to sue.

- *Protect your assets from disgruntled relatives.* It is more difficult to challenge a living trust than a will. Nevertheless, a relative can challenge a trust on grounds of fraud, undue influence or duress.

COMMON TYPES OF IRREVOCABLE TRUSTS

*Asset protection trusts* are primarily designed to shelter assets from creditors or lawsuits, but they can serve other trust purposes. Currently, 10 states permit some type of asset protection trusts.

*Charitable trusts* can save taxes and make distributions to one or more charities during life and after death. A number of variations exist, including *split-interest trusts*, some of which make lifetime payments to one or more individuals.

*Children's trusts* hold assets for a child, for example, until he turns age 21.

COMMON TYPES OF IRREVOCABLE TRUSTS *(continued)*

*Credit shelter trusts* are used to eliminate or reduce federal estate taxes and are typically used by individuals whose estate exceeds the available federal estate tax exemption.

*Dynasty trusts* (a type of generation-skipping trust) stay in effect for generations and are beneficial to the more affluent who want to control trust distributions through future generations.

*Generation-skipping trusts* create a tax-efficient way to pass wealth to grandchildren. Generation-skipping trusts can also make payments first to children, and then to grandchildren.

*Incentive trusts* give the trustee discretion to make distributions based on the beneficiary's performance, such as gainful employment, educational accomplishment or philanthropic pursuit. Some parents establish incentive trusts that require children to conform to desired standards in order to receive their inheritance.

*Irrevocable life insurance trusts* save estate taxes by removing insurance proceeds from the taxable estate.

*Marital trusts* include **QTIP trusts** and *general power of appointment trusts*, which provide income, and principal to a varying extent, to a surviving spouse typically until she dies.

*Special needs trusts* are intended for individuals with disabilities who do not want to be disqualified from receiving governmental benefits.

*Spendthrift trusts* protect inheritances made to 'spendthrift' beneficiaries and may also be useful for lawsuit/creditor protection.

### 5. *What is a power of appointment and how might it be used?*

In addition to providing for distributions to named beneficiaries, trust provisions may also grant a *power of appointment*. By granting a *power of appointment,* you allow the power holder to direct the transfer of property held in an irrevocable trust, either during life (an *inter vivos* power of appointment) or by will (a *testamentary* power of appointment). The terms of the power of appointment may be very broad – allowing the power holder to transfer property to herself or her estate – or they may be narrow, e.g., allowing the power holder to transfer property only to a limited class of beneficiaries.

> **Example:** Mary's documents create a marital trust for her husband John. The terms of the marital trust give John an inter vivos general power of appointment, i.e., during his lifetime he can direct the transfer of trust assets to himself or to others as he chooses.

> **Example:** Mary's documents create an irrevocable trust for her son Charles. Under the terms of the trust, Charles has a testamentary limited power of appointment, e.g., in his will, he can direct the transfer of trust assets only to his descendants or to charity.

As illustrated in the "John" example, a power of appointment may be used in a marital trust to give the surviving spouse more flexibility and control. In other situations (such as in the "Charles" example), it serves to further limit a beneficiary's control over trust assets. Structured properly, powers of appointment can provide flexibility to beneficiaries, without adverse tax consequence.

There is no requirement to include a power of appointment in a trust. Some clients decide not to use them at all, preferring instead to provide only for the distribution of trust assets to designated beneficiaries at the end of the trust term. You will want to talk with your advisors about whether powers of appointment should be included in your wealth transfer plan.

### 6. What is involved in setting up a trust?

Once you've had a thorough discussion with your advisors, your estate planning attorney will be the professional responsible for drafting your trust – a complex, exacting task. You'll probably be asked to review first and second drafts before signing the final version. Ask your attorney to provide a plain language summary to aid your review; check for basics such as distribution provisions, trustee provisions and beneficiary names.

Depending on your state of domicile and the type of document, certain formalities (e.g., witnesses, notarization) may be required to make your arrangements legally binding. Typically, your attorney will retain one of the signed documents for her records; the other copies should be placed in a clearly identifiable file with your other important papers. If you have named a corporate fiduciary as trustee or successor trustee, a copy should also be provided to it.

At this point, you are ready to fund your trust by transferring assets to it. Although your advisors will give you detailed funding directions, it is ultimately your responsibility to make sure the transfers actually occur. Failure to fund a trust – which includes retitling assets – can pose a serious threat to the effectiveness of your wealth transfer plan.

**7.** ***I am the trustee of my revocable trust. What will happen if
I become disabled or die?***

Upon disability or death, the successor trustee you've named
– typically either your spouse, another individual or a corporate
trustee – will assume responsibility for carrying out the terms
of your trust.

For example, if you become disabled, the successor or co-
trustee will step in to manage trust assets and make payments
on behalf of you and your family as directed in the document.
During your period of disability, the acting trustee will not have
the power to amend or revoke your trust, except to the extent
permitted by the document.

At your death, your revocable trust becomes irrevocable, i.e.,
it cannot be amended or revoked by anyone. At that time, the
successor trustee will oversee the orderly distribution of trust
assets to your designated beneficiaries, whether individuals,
charities or trusts for their benefit.

# PART THREE

# WEALTH TRANSFER STRATEGIES

# CHAPTER SEVEN

# Lifetime Gifting Strategies

*When you transfer property while you are living, you remove not only the current value of the asset from your estate, but future appreciation as well. As a result, some of the most effective wealth transfers occur during your lifetime. In this chapter, you will learn which assets are best suited to lifetime gifting and what strategies offer the greatest opportunity to reduce taxes.*

## 1. *When and how should I transfer wealth?*

To determine when and how your beneficiaries should receive your assets, you need to focus on three factors:

- The size and liquidity of your estate versus your need for cash flow during your lifetime;
- The age and maturity of the beneficiaries; and
- The tax implications.

Outright transfers may seem simple, but can create complex problems. For example, an outright transfer to a second spouse may leave children from a prior marriage unprotected. A substantial outright transfer to a young adult could have unintended consequences. In contrast, a trust, by establishing standards for discretionary payments, can adapt income or principal distributions for whatever situation arises.

By setting out the guidelines for trust distributions in advance, a well-drafted document can help protect beneficiaries and assist them in making good financial decisions. Finally, many types of transfer tax planning – including those that make use of the gift, estate and generation-skipping tax exemptions – are particularly well suited to assets held in trust.

## 2. *How can lifetime gifting reduce my taxable estate?*

Even with maximum use of estate tax exemptions and deductions, you may still have considerable estate tax exposure. An effective, popular way to reduce a taxable estate is to transfer assets *before* you die through lifetime gifting.

Lifetime gifting gives you the enjoyment of seeing your recipient benefit from the gift. Because it shifts assets out of your taxable estate before they appreciate further, lifetime gifting leverages the use of your gift tax exemption.

The annual gift tax exclusion allows individuals to gift as much as $12,000 per year (in 2008) to as many people as they wish without gift tax consequences and without depleting the gift or estate tax exemption. As an example, suppose you are married, with three children and six grandchildren. You could give them each $12,000 annually, for a total of $108,000, without tax implications. Your spouse could *also* make gifts and double the amount, which would transfer $216,000 a year from your taxable estate!

For this annual exclusion to apply, the donor must gift a *present* interest in the property to the recipient. This usually means giving the recipient access to the funds.

### 3. *Why might I want to consider making lifetime gifts to my spouse?*

Does your spouse have sufficient assets? If she were to predecease you, would her available estate tax exemption amount be fully utilized? If not, you may want to consider making lifetime transfers to her, either outright or in a properly structured marital trust.

> **Example:** Judy has a small investment portfolio worth $600,000 while her husband Stewart has assets in excess of $5 million. If Judy were to predecease Stewart in 2008, $1.4 million of her available estate tax exemption would be unused. This under-utilization of Judy's exemption could cost $630,000 in additional federal estate tax.

> **Example:** Stewart gifts $1.4 million to Judy so that her total assets equal $2 million. If Judy predeceases Stewart in 2008, the entire $2 million will be sheltered from estate tax by her estate tax exemption. *And if her wealth transfer plan provides for a $2 million credit shelter trust, no part of that trust will be taxed in Stewart's estate either.*

See Chapter Eight for further discussion of marital and credit shelter trusts.

### 4. *Which assets are best to gift?*

Gifts need not be cash; you can gift any asset. But you will save the most in estate taxes by gifting assets that have the greatest potential for future appreciation.

> **Example:** You give your daughter, Allison, a $20,000 bond that during the next five years generates $1,400 of income annually, but does not appreciate in value. After five years, she'll have $27,000 worth of assets that would otherwise have been part of your taxable estate.

> **Example:** Suppose, instead, you give Allison $20,000 in stock that generates no dividends over the next five years, but doubles in value. You have effectively gifted your daughter $20,000 of assets while removing $40,000 (your original gift plus its appreciation) from your taxable estate.

## 5. Are there special ways to gift to a minor for educational purposes?

The gift tax provides an unlimited exclusion for direct payments of tuition (see Chapter Five). Making annual exclusion gifts to Section 529 plans is another option. A 529 Plan allows the contributions to grow on an income tax-deferred basis. Withdrawals used for qualified higher education expenses are also free of income tax.

You could also establish an irrevocable trust. For example, you can create a Section 2503(c) minor's trust specifying that the trust's income and principal be used solely for the benefit of the child until he or she reaches age 21. After that, any remaining income and principal pass to the child. This special type of trust qualifies for the annual gift tax exclusion even though the child has no immediate access to the funds. One disadvantage, however, is that the child *must* be given an opportunity to access the trust assets at age 21.

## 6. What is a family limited partnership? Under what circumstances will a family limited partnership reduce transfer taxes?

Family limited partnerships (FLPs) can be effective tools for asset management, facilitating pooling of investments and economies of scale. If properly structured and administered, they also allow you to remove a substantial percentage of the value of the partnership assets from your taxable estate.

Some of the more common assets that are transferred into FLPs include:

- Real estate;

- Closely held stock;

- Marketable securities; and

- Other limited partnership interests.

### How an FLP works

After funding, the donors will usually gift part or all of their partnership interests to other family members. If the interest being gifted is a limited partnership interest or a non-controlling general partnership interest, minority discounts and discounts for lack of marketability typically reduce substantially the appraised value of each gift. Assuming the donors relinquish control of the partnership prior to death, their gross estate will include only the discounted value of the minority partnership interests that they retain at the date of death.

## 7. How can a grantor retained annuity trust (GRAT) be used to transfer wealth?

A GRAT is a type of trust designed to transfer wealth during your lifetime. Appreciating assets are placed in an irrevocable trust that requires fixed annual payments to the grantor. The payments are based on a number of variables such as the Section 7520 rate, the trust term and the expected growth rate of the assets in the GRAT. At the expiration of the trust term, the remainder is paid to the designated beneficiary – for example, a child – either outright or in trust. Because the payments to the remainder beneficiaries are deferred to the future, the value of the taxable gift (which is determined when

> The **Section 7520 Rate** is published monthly by the IRS and is used to determine the present value of an annuity, an interest for life or for a term of years.

the assets are transferred to the trust) is minimized. Moreover, if the GRAT assets have a higher rate of return than the Section 7520 rate, the actual value of the remainder will exceed the amount subject to gift tax. These are sophisticated vehicles that require careful planning and expert estate planning counsel.

*Note: If the grantor dies before the expiration of the GRAT, part or all of its value will be includable in his estate.*

### 8. What is a qualified personal residence trust (QPRT)?

A qualified personal residence trust (QPRT) holds your personal residence while giving you the right to live in it for a number of years. At the end of the term, the home passes to the remainder beneficiaries named in the trust document (typically your children) or is held in trust for their benefit.

> Possibly the most popular use of the QPRT is for a second or vacation home.

When you transfer your home to a QPRT, you remove it from your taxable estate as long as you survive the trust term. In addition, the QPRT 'freezes' the value of the home at its present value for gift tax purposes. Because a QPRT is a lifetime transfer, your beneficiaries will not receive a step-up in basis when they receive the home. Therefore, they could face an income tax liability when they sell it.

> The tax rules allow you to continue to live in your home at the end of the trust term – as long as you pay a fair market rent.

For income tax purposes, the grantor is considered the owner of the home during the trust term and can claim deductions for real estate taxes and mortgage interest.

A QPRT may be a good idea if you do not anticipate living in the home beyond the trust term, if the home is expected to appreciate in value and if your beneficiaries want to eventually own the home.

*Note:* *If the grantor dies before the expiration of the QPRT, part or all of its value will be includable in her estate.*

# Beyond Lifetime Gifting

*Since it is likely that the estate tax will be with us for years to come, you will want to take advantage of strategies that will reduce the taxes your estate will owe. Chapter Eight explores how you can maximize the amount that goes to your beneficiaries – be they a spouse, your children, a non-family member or a charity.*

### 1. How much can I transfer at death without paying estate tax?

There are unlimited estate tax deductions for properly structured transfers to a spouse or to charity. In addition, anyone can transfer an amount equal to their available estate tax exemption (up to $2 million in 2008) to an individual who is not a spouse. Transfers that do not qualify for the unlimited marital or charitable deduction may be shielded from estate tax by the estate tax exemption.

> **Example:** Harry dies in 2008 with a $2 million estate. His wealth transfer documents provide for a $2 million bequest to his niece Sarah. The $2 million estate tax exemption shelters his entire $2 million estate from estate tax.

### 2. I am married and have a $3 million estate. How can I use my available estate tax exemption amount to provide for my spouse and children?

Credit shelter trusts (also called Bypass, "B" or family trusts) are funded with an amount up to the estate tax exemption amount and are typically used when the husband's or wife's estate will exceed the amount exempt from federal estate tax.

Depending on your objectives, a credit shelter trust can be used to benefit:

- A surviving spouse;

- A surviving spouse and your children;

- Your children alone; or

- Anyone else.

**Example:** John, who lives in a common law state, has a $4 million estate. His wealth transfer plan provides that assets equal to the exemption amount ($2 million) fund a separate trust on his death. The protection that this 'credit shelter trust' offers his wife Mary can be substantial, including mandatory income, discretionary principal and a limited withdrawal right. The remaining assets ($2 million) pass directly to Mary and qualify for the unlimited marital deduction. At Mary's death, whatever remains in the credit shelter trust passes to other family members without estate tax.

Under the estate tax rules, the $2 million credit shelter trust is not in Mary's estate when she dies. As a result, Mary and John save a significant amount of federal estate taxes and are able to pass much more to their beneficiaries.

### 3. I am married. How can the marital deduction reduce my estate taxes?

For married couples, the unlimited marital deduction is one of the most powerful estate planning tools. Any assets passing to a surviving spouse pass tax-free at the time the first spouse dies, *as long as the surviving spouse is a U.S. citizen* and the transfer is properly structured.

You can take full advantage of the unlimited marital deduction by making outright gifts or bequests, titling assets in joint tenancy with rights of survivorship or tenancy by the entirety, naming a spouse as the beneficiary of life insurance or retirement plan proceeds, or transferring assets to a trust that qualifies for the unlimited marital deduction.

### 4. Since the marital deduction is unlimited, why shouldn't I leave everything to my spouse?

If you or your spouse's estate will exceed the available exemption amount, it will be necessary to use the estate tax exemptions of both spouses.

**Example:** Michele and Daniel, who are married and live in a common law state, have a combined estate of $4 million, of which $3 million is titled to Daniel and $1 million is titled to Michele. At Daniel's death in 2008, his assets pass to Michele – estate-tax free because of the unlimited marital deduction. Daniel thus has no taxable estate. Michele dies the same year leaving a $4 million estate. The first $2 million is exempt from estate tax because of her exemption amount. But the remaining $2 million is subject to federal estate tax of roughly $900,000.

In this example, Michele and Daniel failed to take advantage of the $2 million exemption in each estate.

**Alternative:** Same facts as above, except Daniel's documents provide that $2 million be used to fund a credit shelter trust that pays income and principal to Michele. When Michele dies, the credit shelter trust is not included in her estate. As a result, her $2 million estate is completely sheltered by the $2 million estate tax exemption available in 2008 and the couple's full $4 million in assets pass to their beneficiaries free of estate tax.

### 5. Can a transfer to an irrevocable trust for the benefit of a spouse qualify for the marital exemption?

A properly structured marital trust (also known as an "A" trust) will qualify for the marital deduction and typically is funded with assets that *exceed* the estate tax exemption amount.

- One alternative is a qualified terminable interest property (QTIP) trust that provides income and discretionary principal to your spouse during her lifetime – and then distributes to beneficiaries selected by you. This type of arrangement is a frequent choice where there are children from a first marriage – or where the surviving spouse is not financially sophisticated.

- Another alternative, which gives the surviving spouse maximum control, is the *general power of appointment trust.* This type of trust gives the surviving spouse the power to withdraw or transfer trust assets during life, at death or both.

Any assets remaining in either a QTIP or general power of appointment trust will be includable in the surviving spouse's estate and may be taxed at his death.

### 6. What about non-citizen spouses? Are they subject to special tax rules?

The unlimited marital deduction is generally not available to a surviving spouse who is not a U.S. citizen. A limited exception exists for transfers to a *qualified domestic trust* (QDOT) that meets special requirements. Any principal distributions from a QDOT to the non-citizen spouse during her life and any assets remaining in the QDOT at her death will be subject to federal estate tax. An exception exists for "hardship" distributions if there is an immediate and substantial financial need, e.g., the spouse's health, maintenance, education or support.

### 7. Given the risk of divorce, what steps should be considered to protect assets?

Although many families with substantial wealth choose to take some preventative measures, the effectiveness of any strategy will depend on factors as diverse as judicial temperament, the circumstances surrounding the dissolution of the marriage and governing state law.

For example, where there is substantial inherited wealth, one common technique is to place at least a portion of those assets in an irrevocable trust. Then, if the divorcing couple cannot agree on the proper division of assets, the divorce court may focus only on marital property held outside the trust. However, the story usually does not end there. In most states, the court can take into account resources held separately from the marital property when determining the proper amount of child support or spousal maintenance. In some states, the court can even order the payment of child support – or spousal maintenance – from an irrevocable trust.

As an alternative, some couples may want to consider using a pre-marital agreement to clarify what each party is bringing into the marriage and to provide for the distribution of property in the event of divorce or death. Although this may be useful in some circumstances, a pre-marital agreement is generally given weight only if its terms are fundamentally fair and both sides are represented by counsel. In some circumstances, courts may refuse to give any weight at all to these agreements.

**8. Are there any special tax strategies for those in second marriages?**

Wealth transfer planning for a second marriage can be more complicated – especially when there are children from a prior marriage. Finding the right planning technique for your situation can ease family tensions, provide for a surviving spouse and also help you pass more assets to your children with fewer tax implications.

A QTIP marital trust can maximize estate tax deferral, while providing for both the surviving spouse and the children from a prior marriage.

**Example:** At Sam's death, a QTIP trust is created for his second wife Elaine. During her life, Elaine receives income and discretionary payments from principal. At Elaine's death, the trust distributes to Sam's children from his first marriage.

**9. I am not married. What tax strategies are available?**

For single individuals, as for married couples, the basic question is: "To whom should I transfer my wealth?" There may be children, grandchildren, nephews, nieces and unrelated individuals. You may be concerned about aging parents, a partner, a less-well-off sibling or a long-time significant other. Before you begin to consider tax strategies, first consider your potential beneficiaries – including charities you wish to benefit.

Without a marital deduction, it is even more important for single individuals to reduce their taxable estates by making sensible and effective use of lifetime gifting strategies. Possibilities range from simple annual exclusion gifts to complex structures such as family limited partnerships (see Chapter Seven). An additional opportunity is offered by the unlimited charitable deduction under both the gift tax and the estate tax. Techniques like charitable gift annuities and charitable remainder trusts allow you to benefit both charity and one or more individual beneficiaries, while reducing your overall estate tax burden (see Chapter Fifteen).

Like single individuals, unmarried couples are also not allowed the benefit of the unlimited marital deduction and face a similarly overwhelming estate tax burden. Once again, the key is using available tax reduction solutions, such as traditional annual gifting, creating an irrevocable life insurance trust or establishing a charitable remainder trust to benefit the other partner.

## 10. How can I protect my wealth from creditors and potential lawsuits?

If you do not protect your assets from creditors and from potential lawsuits during your lifetime, you could be vulnerable. This is particularly true if you are a professional or business owner.

Insurance, state and federal statutes and asset placement can all work together.

- Insurance provides protection against losses from malpractice claims, casualty losses and personal injury claims.

- Certain federal and state laws provide some statutory protection: creditors can't enforce a lien or judgment against property that is exempt under federal or state law.

- Asset placement involves transferring legal ownership of assets to other persons or entities, such as corporations, limited partnerships and trusts – creditors may find it more difficult to reach property that you do not own or control.

In Chapter Six, we mentioned that several states permit asset protection trusts – a trust primarily designed to shelter assets from creditors or lawsuits. In essence, these states permit the creation of an irrevocable trust of which you, the grantor, are a beneficiary, retaining various interests in, and powers over, the trust. Despite your continuing interest in potential distributions of income and principal from the trust, your creditors will not be able to satisfy their claims from its assets unless they can timely establish that the funding of the trust amounted to a fraudulent transfer.

> A substantial number of grantors of asset protection trusts are physicians, who use this type of trust to protect a portion of their wealth against excess, uninsured liabilities. This strategy is also used by corporate directors who have concerns about their personal liability for uninsured claims arising out of shareholder litigation.

Asset protection is a very complex area of wealth transfer planning. If you are concerned about your exposure to potential lawsuits or creditors, you should meet with your wealth transfer team to assess your situation and identify the appropriate solutions to meet your needs.

### 11. *What is a spendthrift trust?*

An anti-alienation or spendthrift clause attempts to protect the trust's assets from the beneficiary's creditors by prohibiting the trustee from transferring trust assets to anyone other than the beneficiary, including creditors.

A spendthrift clause does not always provide a beneficiary with absolute protection. For example, several states do not fully enforce spendthrift provisions. Additionally, a spendthrift clause may not completely protect a beneficiary from bankruptcy, divorce or tax claims. Nor does it protect income distributions already received.

An additional protective measure is to grant the trustee maximum discretionary powers, including the right to withhold income and principal payments whenever the trustee believes the funds would be claimed by the beneficiary's creditors.

### 12. *Does charitable gifting play an important role in reducing estate taxes?*

Direct bequests to charity are fully deductible for estate tax purposes. If you leave your entire estate to charity (or an amount that reduces your estate to the available exemption amount), you'll pay no estate taxes.

If you want to make a partial transfer to charity and a partial transfer to individual beneficiaries, a trust can be the answer. There are many types of charitable trusts which can be designed to meet your specific goals and tax situation. The appropriate trust will depend upon your current needs, your beneficiaries' needs, your estate's composition and your charitable intentions.

You'll learn more about how philanthropy can reduce estate taxes in Chapter Fifteen.

# PART FOUR

# PLANNING FOR SPECIAL ASSETS

# Planning for Retirement Assets

*The potential tax burden on retirement assets is high – as high as 70% when both estate and income tax are taken into account. Chapter Nine looks at this important component of your estate and explains why a carefully crafted beneficiary designation is a critical part of your wealth transfer plan. Pay special attention to the discussion of disclaimers.*

1.  ***How do I transfer my retirement assets?***

    Retirement assets pass at your death to beneficiaries named by you in a separate document, a "beneficiary designation," generally a form provided by the custodian or trustee of the plan or account. You cannot use your will or revocable trust to transfer assets such as individual retirement accounts and qualified plans. Like other types of property with "built-in beneficiary designations," these assets will not be subject to probate.

2.  ***Can you explain beneficiary designations?***

    The beneficiary designation states who will receive the retirement plan proceeds. You will need to choose one or more primary beneficiaries and one or more contingent beneficiaries; the contingent beneficiaries will receive the proceeds if the primary beneficiaries either predecease you or disclaim (i.e., refuse to accept) the retirement benefits in whole or in part. If you do not name contingent beneficiaries, proceeds may pass to your estate.

3.  ***Why is it important to think about taxes when making beneficiary designations?***

    The fair market value of your retirement plans is included in your estate and is subject to estate tax. In addition, distributions from retirement accounts to your beneficiaries are generally taxed to them as ordinary income. Properly structured beneficiary designations can save or defer taxes by stretching out the time period over which required distributions are made (the "payout period"), since distributions are not taxed until distributed. One option, if you are married, is to name your spouse as beneficiary. Assuming you predecease your spouse, she can roll over your qualified plan or IRA into a new IRA, naming your children as beneficiaries. A new payout period will start at your death and again at the death of your spouse – stretching out the payment period.

### 4. How can I be sure my beneficiary designations accomplish my goals?

Your beneficiary designations are an important part of your wealth transfer plan and should be reviewed whenever your plan is reviewed (see Chapter One). First, check with the plan sponsor, custodian or trustee to determine what designations are currently in place. Next, have your estate planning attorney review your current designations as the technical rules are complex and it takes an expert to maximize all potential tax benefits. Finally, work with your estate planning attorney to update your beneficiary designations as circumstances and tax laws change. Again, communication is critical. For example, children who have become independently wealthy may prefer that you minimize potential transfer tax by naming your grandchildren (or trusts for your grandchildren) as retirement plan beneficiaries. In other situations, you may decide to name a charity as a primary or contingent beneficiary.

### 5. What distribution options are available to beneficiaries of my plans?

Beneficiaries generally have only two distribution options – take a lump-sum distribution or take payments equal to at least the required minimum distribution (RMD) each year. The RMD is based on the IRS actuarial table for the life expectancy of the beneficiary. The annual distribution is the account balance divided by the beneficiary's expected remaining years of life, allowing a young beneficiary to stretch the distributions in installments over several decades.

Many beneficiaries prefer RMD installment payments rather than lump-sum distribution because a lump-sum distribution may put them in a higher tax bracket. With installment payments, a beneficiary can choose to take only the RMD, allowing the balance to grow tax-deferred. Income taxes are payable only on distributions, not on the overall value of the account.

> **A DISCLAIMER CAN BE USEFUL IN A NUMBER OF SITUATIONS**
>
> - If a beneficiary already has a large estate, a disclaimer will keep the property out of his estate and avoid the potential increase in estate tax.
>
> - If the primary beneficiary is in a high income tax bracket when income-producing property is left to him – and the contingent beneficiary is his child – he may want to disclaim the property if his child is in a lower income tax bracket.

There is a third option – a named beneficiary can choose to "disclaim" all or a portion of his share of the retirement account, i.e., refuse to accept some or all of the benefits from the account. A disclaimer is a valuable estate planning tool that allows a gift tax-free redistribution of assets after your death. If a beneficiary disclaims, he is treated as having predeceased the decedent, so that the property passes directly to the contingent beneficiaries. The disclaimant is regarded as never having received the property.

*Note: Disclaimers must be carefully drafted by an estate planning attorney. To be effective for tax purposes, they must be delivered to the custodian or trustee within nine months after the date of death. In addition, the disclaimant cannot benefit from the disclaimed property in any way.*

**6.  Should I name a trust as the beneficiary of a retirement account?**

In some situations, it makes sense to name a trust as beneficiary of your retirement accounts. For example, a trust may prove useful in the following situations:

- Perhaps you are concerned that a designated beneficiary is unsophisticated or ill-equipped to handle a significant inheritance – and will therefore take distributions too quickly. You may decide to establish a trust with explicit distribution instructions, administered by a knowledgeable trustee.

- A *special needs trust* can be funded with your retirement benefits to provide for a disabled beneficiary (see Chapter Twelve).

- In a blended family situation, assets are frequently left to the surviving spouse in a special type of marital trust (see discussion of QTIP trust in Chapter Eight); your documents may provide that your retirement plans will be used to fund that trust in whole or in part.

These arrangements can work well – as long as you coordinate your plans for beneficiary designations with a knowledgeable estate planning attorney who is familiar with your plan and the rules governing retirement planning.

### 7. *Should I name a charity as a primary or contingent beneficiary of a retirement account?*

Selecting which assets to transfer to charity is an important step in maximizing the impact of your philanthropy. Traditional retirement assets, with their built-in income tax liability, are generally a great choice for charitable giving. *(**Note:** Roth IRAs, which do not have any built-in income tax liability, are an exception to this rule.)* Among the most frequently used strategies are:

- Naming one or more charities as the sole beneficiaries. As a variation on this theme, you might choose to name a donor advised fund, private foundation or charitable remainder trust as sole beneficiary. More sophisticated planning is needed if you choose to leave part of a retirement account to charity and part to individuals.

- Naming a charity as a contingent beneficiary, with an individual beneficiary as primary beneficiary. If, at your death, the individual beneficiary chooses to disclaim the retirement benefits, in whole or in part, the charity will receive the disclaimed portion. The advantage of this approach is its flexibility; the disadvantage is that your charitable plan is dependent on the choices made by the individual beneficiary.

# CHAPTER TEN

# Planning for Unique Assets

*The disposition and division of tangible personal property and real estate can create conflict in even the most harmonious of families. Thoughtful planning for unique assets can be an important part of your legacy.*

## 1. Why might I decide to leave different assets to different recipients?

Whether for personal, tax or business reasons, you may want to be sure that certain property goes to a particular recipient. For instance, you may want to gift a prized collection to the child who will keep it intact. Similarly, a daughter helping her dad run the family business is a likely choice to receive company stock. One child wants the vacant land that the family has owned for many years, and another always loved the summer home. Items of less significant monetary value (dad's fishing gear or mom's piano) can be significant emotionally. Aligning your plans for unique assets with your beneficiaries' expectations can help to minimize conflict.

### Avoiding family conflicts

Most parents leave personal items and household contents equally to their children, confident that they can harmoniously divide the assets among themselves. Too often, however, instructions to divide personal effects stir strong emotions.

Leaving specific objects to specific children or other beneficiaries can be better accomplished by:

- Making a gift while you are alive;

- Making a bequest of specific items in your will; or

- Having a skilled executor who can select an appropriate method of distribution (e.g., an "auction" or a round-robin selection) to facilitate orderly division.

*Equalizing gifts*

Even if your plan includes specific bequests, you may still be able to equalize transfers among beneficiaries with cash, insurance or other property. Skilled drafting will prevent fluctuating values from presenting a potential problem.

2. **What should I consider when contemplating transfer of the family home?**

When planning for the disposition of the family home, take into account your children's emotions as well as their finances.

- Unlike money in a savings account, a home cannot be easily divided among the children.

- One child may want to keep – even live in – the home, while his siblings may want the home sold.

- If the home is transferred to one child, his siblings may feel shortchanged, even if they have received other assets of equivalent value.

- If the home needs repairs or has maintenance costs, one or more of the children may not be able to contribute financially.

- Legal complications may arise if a child with a judgment or tax lien inherits the home.

One option is to bequeath the home to the child who wants it, and provide that assets of equivalent value be transferred to your other children. If other assets are not sufficient to equalize distributions, life insurance could be purchased for this purpose. Alternatively, one child can buy the home from the estate.

### Special considerations for blended families

Blended families can generate additional challenges. For example, you may not want your home – or its contents – to pass immediately to your children from a prior marriage. You can provide for your surviving spouse with a QTIP trust.

3. **What are some alternatives for disposition of the family vacation home?**

Vacation homes often play a unique role in a family's well being; they can continue to do so for several generations, with proper planning. Your plan should consider:

- The appropriate vehicle to facilitate tax efficient transfer (e.g., an FLP, LLC or trust) and proper management;

- How use of the home will be shared among family members;

- How the home's expenses will be allocated; and

- How decisions about the home's operation will be made.

An endowment to cover operating expenses and upkeep and a governance structure for decision making are excellent tools to facilitate long-term shared use with minimal conflict. (For a discussion of QPRTs, see Chapter Seven).

SITUATION: VACATION HOME.

When they were younger, James and Martha spent every summer on their vacation ranch in the Cascade Mountains of Washington State. Now residents of Arizona (which has no estate tax), the couple has decided to pass the property on to their children, who are now grown.

When they share their plans over Thanksgiving dinner, they learn, much to their surprise, that the children do not have fond memories of the ranch and have no interest in owning it.

Uncertain what to do next, the couple sets up a meeting with their estate planning attorney and their accountant. They are shocked to learn that the appraised value of the property exceeds $2 million and that Washington State has its own estate tax.

SOLUTION

After talking with their advisors, James and Martha sell the property, transferring the net proceeds to a family limited partnership, with interests held by each family member. The partnership invests the proceeds in a diversified portfolio. James and Martha use their partnership distributions to take a long-postponed trip to Paris. The children use their partnership distributions to pay college tuition for the grandchildren.

Their eldest child, an accountant, serves as general partner and makes sure that the partnership is properly administered.

Over time, James and Martha gift all of their partnership interests to their children. They pay no gift tax on the transfers, which are shielded from tax by the couple's annual gift tax exclusions and lifetime gift tax exemptions.

Because they no longer own the Washington ranch, James and Martha pay no Washington estate tax. Moreover, because of their lifetime gifts, no part of the partnership's appreciated value is subject to federal estate tax in their estates.

**4.** *What special issues arise with limited partnership interests?*

As a limited partner, you may be subject to certain restrictions on the transferability of your limited partnership interest. For example, you may be allowed to transfer your interest only at certain times – and only to certain classes of individuals, such as family members. In addition, consent of the general partner may be required before a transfer is valid, and your transferee may be required to agree to the terms of the existing partnership agreement. For all these reasons, you will want to have your advisors review the underlying partnership agreement and partnership transfer documents to be sure that a transfer is both permissible and legally binding as executed – and that your transferee receives all the rights of a successor limited partner.

**5.** *What special issues arise with other intangible assets such as oil and gas interests, intellectual property and notes receivable?*

Special assets often require special technical expertise. With non-publicly traded intangibles, identifying the asset and understanding your ownership interest is the key. Because of their complexity and the need to monitor income collection closely, it's usually best to put these assets in trust so they are not forgotten. A knowledgeable trustee is critical.

**6.** *What are some alternatives for disposition of real estate investments?*

A great deal will depend upon how the real estate is titled and who controls the ultimate ownership interest. For instance, investment properties can be owned by limited liability companies (LLCs) or limited partnerships (LPs). These entities may, in turn, be owned by one or more trusts. What a trustee can do with the property depends on the terms of the trust and the partnership agreement or company operating agreement. If the real estate is tied to a business, you will need to consider how its transfer would affect the business. Sometimes, commercial real estate can be worth considerably more than the actual business that occupies the property.

Alternatively, several family members might own an interest in the property. Wealth transfer planning then shifts to the preparation of a buy-sell agreement, i.e., an agreement among the current owners about ownership in the event of death or disability. Buy-sell agreements are often funded with life insurance.

### *Transferring real estate to a charitable remainder trust*
Many donors choose to contribute appreciated real estate to charitable remainder trusts during their lifetime. This strategy can provide cash flow and defer capital gains tax. As long as the remainder beneficiary of the charitable remainder trust is a public charity, the charitable deduction will be based on the property's fair market value. In many cases, a flip unitrust (see Chapter Fifteen) is a particularly appropriate vehicle.

7. *How should I handle my collection of art (or antique cars, rare books, etc.)?*

Many collectors find it difficult to consider parting with a collection of art, coins or other valuable, tangible personal property. But unless disposition is carefully thought through, individual pieces may not be properly preserved and maintained after the owner's death – or the collection as a whole may be dispersed.

If you are considering passing your collectibles to your children or other family members, be sure to consider also their interest in the collection, their ability to properly display or store it, and whether they have the financial resources to pay substantial insurance premiums.

Another issue is estate taxes. A valuable, but illiquid, collection can create an estate tax nightmare – i.e., a substantial tax liability with insufficient cash to pay the tax. An alternative is to remove the collection from your taxable estate.

In the right situation, a well-planned gift to charity (such as a museum or university) – either during life or at death – may be the answer. In general, early communication with the recipient charity is critical. It is important to verify, for example, that the intended recipient wants the collection and has the resources to assume responsibility for it. If a charity is unable or unwilling to accept the gift, it is important to know sooner rather than later.

# CHAPTER ELEVEN

# Planning for the Family Business

*As a business owner, you face unique challenges relating to leadership succession, estate taxes and liquidity. What you do now – or fail to do – will determine whether your business survives. This chapter focuses on how timely planning can effectively address your concerns, protecting both your business and your family.*

1. ***What special issues are raised when a business is a major part of the family's assets?***

Business owners must plan for the continuity, management and possible sale of their business if they die or become disabled. They must identify and designate business successors, and decide when and how to sell or transition the business as tax-efficiently as possible. They must also know how to position the business so that it maintains maximum value.

If you are a business owner, some of the special questions and issues you will need to address include:

- How much is the business worth?

- Are there partners who may want to buy your interest?

- What employees or family members can run the business if you die or become incapacitated?

- Does your family want to sell or retain the business?

- Should you sell or transfer the business to your children now or later?

- How can your family retain the value of the business and ensure its continuity?

- Are you concerned about the effect that claims against your business could have on you personally?

Be sure also to explore these issues with your family and partners. Consider how *their* views might influence *your* decisions.

## *Sale of a family business*

If you decide that your business should be sold at your death, assuring that survivors will receive a fair price will be a concern. Of course, much depends on the nature, condition and salability of the business, the spouse's or family's capacity to manage the business, and whether successor management is in place or can be quickly put in place.

Because family owned businesses are not publicly traded, their exact value can be difficult to determine. While you may feel you have a good sense of the value of your business, a formal valuation can be a useful tool in assessing strategic alternatives.

Think about whether you want to:

- Sell the business during your lifetime and invest the proceeds for the benefit of your beneficiaries. This could be of interest if you are an older business owner without good succession alternatives. The most sensible solution may be for you to sell the business – at the best price – as opposed to a distressed sale later. By selling the business while you are alive, you will have locked in its value.

- Use a buy-sell agreement to pre-negotiate the sale of the business to a buyer who would take over ownership at your death. This may be a good solution for the business that has multiple owners or long-standing employees.

If you do not sell your business during your lifetime, take steps to ensure that your estate has the liquidity to pay estate taxes on its value or that the business will qualify for deferred payment of estate taxes.

**2. *I am the owner of a family business. What should I be thinking about <u>now</u> to help with estate tax payments <u>later</u>?***

A successful business can trigger substantial estate taxes. There are a number of methods to cope with the tax issues. Here are three recommendations:

- At appropriate intervals during your lifetime, have a qualified appraiser determine the business' value. Your advisors can then calculate the tax impact on your wealth transfer planning.

- Discuss with your advisors whether your estate will qualify for installment payments. If certain requirements are met, your executor or trustee can choose to pay the federal estate taxes resulting from business ownership over a period of years.

- Determine if your executor or trustee will have enough cash or liquid assets to pay the estate taxes on the business. If not, investigate buying life insurance to cover the expense. Alternatively, consider removing some of its value from your estate by making lifetime gifts of the business to your children or charitable trusts.

SITUATION: CONTEMPLATING FAMILY BUSINESS SUCCESSION.

Harriet, who is divorced, owns a thriving landscaping business, which she runs with the help of her daughter Monica. Her other three children – Tim, Stuart and Julie – are professionals living in other cities. Although Harriet would like to pass the business on to Monica, she would like to provide for her other children as well.

SOLUTION

With her objectives firmly in mind, Harriet sets up a meeting with her estate planning attorney and her accountant. They begin to work together on a family business succession plan that ensures that Monica will own the business at Harriet's death. Among the possibilities they discuss are:

- Selling a portion of the real estate owned by the business and using the proceeds to fund a life insurance trust benefiting the other three children.

- Using life insurance to ensure there is sufficient liquidity to pay estate tax on Harriet's death.

- Using a GRAT to transfer shares of the business to Monica during Harriet's lifetime.

- Transferring shares of the business to Monica in a bargain sale.

- Gifting shares of the business to Monica.

On the recommendation of her planners, Harriet talks frankly with the other children about her intentions. After meeting with their mother, the children come to the conclusion that they are each being treated fairly and agree that Monica should have the business.

By working with her advisors, Harriet has avoided what could have been a bitter family conflict. Communication with all her children was a key component of the planning process.

### 3. How should I decide whether to continue family ownership or sell my business to an unrelated third party?

One way to approach this question is to consider both your own goals and priorities and those of your children.

For example, if your children are active in the business, do they want the responsibility of owning it? Would the business continue to prosper under their ownership?

Let's face it – your children might have other career goals, might not be interested in the business or might not have managerial capability.

Even when capable children do want the business, you may do better financially by selling to a non-family member. A cash sale to a stranger would provide more financial security than a long-term installment note from a child. Of course, there are non-financial factors as well. For instance, will selling to a child necessarily keep you involved in the business longer than you want? Do you prefer a clean and immediate break? Would selling to one child cause conflict with your other children or with your spouse?

### 4. I have three children, but only one is active in the family business. How can I give each child a share of my wealth without giving each ownership of the family business?

If you leave your children equal ownership in the family business, you may be guaranteeing hopeless deadlock. This can hurt the business and cause sibling conflict. On the other hand, unequal ownership means the child owning more shares will have control, which can frustrate the other children who may have their own ideas about proper management, compensation paid to the child employed in the business and earnings distributions.

One solution is to sell the business to the child who works in the business. Although sale proceeds remaining in your estate will be subject to estate tax, future appreciation in the value of the business will escape transfer tax. The children can then equally share your estate when you die.

If you don't want to sell to your child now, you could give that child an option to buy the business at an agreed price in the future or upon your death.

A third alternative is to transfer the business to the working child, leaving other assets of equal value to each of your other children. Life insurance can provide the needed liquidity.

If you are determined to leave your business equally to two or more children, however, take the time now to make sure that they can amicably resolve business disagreements. Test the waters by encouraging your children to make management decisions together while you are alive to observe the outcome.

### 5.  *How can I ensure the orderly transfer of my business to my children?*

A parent's transition of family business ownership to a child or children has a greater likelihood of success if preceded by the formulation of a *management succession plan.* Development of a plan which would provide the child (or children) with experience in the day-to-day management of the business, leading to an eventual assumption by the child of full management responsibility will:

- Provide the child with credibility (to non-family employees, vendors and customers);

- Enable the child to make mistakes and learn from them, without materially impacting the business in a negative way; and

- Allow the parent to evaluate the child's likelihood of succeeding in a senior management role.

While reduction of the parent's estate taxes may be the eventual goal, providing for the ongoing growth and success of the business is, from an overall economic standpoint, even more critical.

**6. *How can I transfer family business interests to family members during my life in a way that reduces estate taxes and allows me to retain control?***

Once the parent has decided upon the timing and recipient(s) of the transfer of his equity interests, there are several planning techniques that can be employed to transfer ownership in a tax effective manner, such as:

- **Use of a grantor retained annuity trust (GRAT).** Contributing an interest in the business to a GRAT is a common planning technique. This strategy provides for the annual payment of an annuity to the grantor (the parent) in cash or in kind for a specified number of years. At the termination of the GRAT, the remaining assets are distributed to the designated beneficiaries (child or children, either outright or in trust).

By taking advantage of certain disparities between the Section 7520 rate and the growth of the business, ownership interests can be transferred to the next generation with minimum gift tax liability. Depending on a number of factors, including the structure of the GRAT and the disposition of voting rights associated with the company stock, a parent could transfer minority interest(s) in the business while retaining voting control.

- **Recapitalization of the business into voting and non-voting equity followed by a planned gifting of the non-voting equity interests.** By utilizing the annual gift tax exclusion and the lifetime gift tax exemption, a parent could, depending on relative values and timing, gift the non-voting interests without incurring income or gift taxes. The voting control would, if desired, remain with the parent.

  > Depending on the circumstances, these techniques can be combined to transfer equity interests in the same business. Each one of these techniques has advantages and disadvantages (including tax outcomes) that need to be weighed against the desired objective. Some of the techniques may carry with them a higher risk of challenge by the IRS, which may result in additional taxes, interest and penalties.

- **Sale of equity interests to an intentionally defective grantor trust (IDGT).** By taking advantage of certain discounts associated with valuing a minority interest in a family business, the grantor (parent) can sell a minority interest in the business to a trust (which has been carefully drafted by the attorney to maximize its tax effectiveness) in exchange for a note. This planning device will enable the parent to immediately transfer equity interests to a trust for the benefit of and eventual receipt by the designated beneficiaries; lock in the lowest valuation for estate tax purposes; avoid payment of income or gift taxes; and retain for himself an annuity stream from repayment of the note.

- **Contribution of equity interests into a family limited partnership followed by a gift of the limited partnership interests.** By utilizing the annual gift tax exclusion and the lifetime gift tax exemption, a parent could, depending on relative values and timing, gift the limited partnership interests without incurring income or gift taxes. The parent would retain the general partner interest, thereby retaining ownership control over the business.

  *Note: If the parent dies holding the general partnership interest, part or all of the assets of the partnership may be included in his estate.*

> **KEEP IN MIND**
>
> - If you hold an interest in your business at your death, your estate is likely to owe estate tax on the value of that interest.
>
> - Congress has drafted tax laws that distinguish between bona fide business arrangements and structures which elevate form over substance. For example, a purported buy-sell agreement that transfers stock to family members at below-market values will be disregarded for purposes of determining the value of the stock for estate or gift tax purposes.

The above techniques are very complex; you should consult with an estate planning attorney familiar with these and other tax planning strategies to determine whether or not a particular vehicle is suitable for your circumstances.

### 7. Under what circumstances does a buy-sell agreement make sense?

Buy-sell agreements are important for those holding interests in multi-owner corporations, limited liability companies, limited partnerships and other business entities with two or more owners. Usually, surviving partners want to continue the business when one partner dies. The most common way to transfer the deceased owner's interest in the business is through a buy-sell agreement where the surviving partner(s) agrees to buy the interest of the deceased partner.

A buy-sell agreement offers three key benefits:

1. It provides a ready market for the shares in the case of disability or in the event the owner's estate wants to sell the stock after the owner's death.

2. It sets a price or determines the methodology for pricing the shares. In the right circumstances, it also fixes the value for estate tax purposes.

3. It provides for stable business continuity by avoiding unnecessary disagreements and lengthy negotiations.

Usually the partners buy life insurance to fund the purchase. Alternatively, the surviving partner can buy the deceased partner's share of the company on financed terms.

### 8. *What factors are important in considering a gradual sale of a business to an employee?*

Before taking on a "partner" in a family business, ask yourself:

- Can you comfortably share managing the business with your new partner?

- What if the co-ownership doesn't work out? Can you buy back your interest? If so, at what price and on what terms?

- What if your employee dies, becomes disabled, goes bankrupt or divorces?

- When will managerial control shift to your employee?

- What safeguards do you have against being forced out of the business?

- When can you or your employee trigger the complete buyout of the business?

Most importantly, ask why you are entering into this arrangement. Is it to motivate your employee to work harder? Is it to provide an incentive in order to retain the employee?

You must be fully confident that the employee will complete the purchase and successfully run the business thereafter. This is particularly important if you are to finance the sale.

### 9. Are ESOPs commonly used when selling shares of a closely held business to employees?

Sale of closely held stock to an employee stock ownership plan ("ESOP") continues to be a popular exit strategy for many business owners, offering potential liquidity, flexibility and tax efficiency.

Once the plan is established, majority owners can decide how much stock to sell – and when – giving them an enviable degree of retained control. For minority owners, sales to the ESOP can create liquidity where there was none before. And for employees, an ESOP may mean not only shared ownership, but also increased participation and productivity. In addition, under special statutory rules, sales of stock to an ESOP by the business owners can be structured to defer tax, sometimes indefinitely.

Although the rules here are complex – you'll need to work with your wealth transfer team on the required technical compliance – the rewards can be great.

### 10. We've been talking about planning for business succession. Is there planning I can do to protect my business in the event I am incapacitated?

The incapacity of the family business owner can cause a serious disruption in the business, including loss of customers as well as valued employees. To deal with such an eventuality, a comprehensive plan will need to be formulated so that the impact of the owner's incapacity is minimized both at the management and owner levels.

At the management level, the family business owner can anticipate and address the vacuum created by her incapacity through formulation of a management succession plan (see pages 115 – 116) which can be drafted to anticipate such an event. The company's bylaws (or other governing documents) and Board actions (or the equivalent) enable the management succession plan to be effective in dealing with this issue as seamlessly as possible.

At the owner level, incapacity can be addressed through appropriate wealth transfer planning techniques such as a revocable trust which shifts responsibility for the voting of equity interests to a successor trustee; depending on circumstances, the use of a voting trust; and/or use of an appropriately customized durable power of attorney.

In the absence of such planning strategies, expensive (and potentially demeaning) guardianship proceedings will be the only way to deal with the incapacity. Because each situation is different, the business owner should seek the advice of an attorney familiar with the array of techniques available.

# PART FIVE

# CREATING A LEGACY

# Transferring Wealth to Children

*Chapter Twelve begins with two basic questions: "How much is enough?" and "Is 'equal treatment' always fair?" We then explore the timing of transfers, both to minors and to adult children. Finally, the chapter examines several strategies we have seen our clients use with success.*

1. *How do I decide how much of my estate to transfer to each child? How much is enough?*

This is a personal decision – one that reflects your values and goals, as much as your finances. Perhaps the question really is "How much is *too much*?" Wealthy parents who can afford to leave their children considerably more, frequently and purposely leave them less. Their hope is to better motivate their children to achieve more on their own.

We've found that parents often want to give their children enough to ensure their financial security. To some, this may mean paying for education. To others, it means helping the children buy a home or business.

To quantify how much is "too much," ask yourself:

- How large is your estate?

- What are your other gifting priorities?

- What are your children's needs based on their age, health, special needs and foreseeable financial situation?

- At what point would a larger inheritance be a disincentive?

- What amount would be most appropriate for your children's growth and happiness?

2. *Is "equal" treatment always "fair?"*

We typically see equality in distribution patterns regardless of sex or age, with more parents adopting the philosophy that unequal economic circumstances do not justify unequal inheritances. These parents view equality as fairness. They assume that their children will see it this way, too.

Only occasionally do we encounter unequal distributions to children, which are usually related to providing incremental funds for a disabled child or a child with a long-term medical condition.

Whatever your philosophy, share it with your children so that they understand the rationale behind your actions. Good communication now can avoid misunderstandings and resentment.

### 3. How can I make a significant gift to a minor during my lifetime?

For families with substantial wealth, significant gifts to minors can be an important part of the wealth transfer plan. From a transfer tax standpoint, the planning goal is to transfer as much wealth as possible over time without paying tax. However, you can't give thousands directly to a toddler – and you wouldn't want to. And, banks and brokers won't establish accounts in the name of your minor alone since minors lack the legal ability to enter into a contract.

Among the potential solutions is a trust with a family member as trustee, or a custodial account created under your state's Uniform Transfers to Minors Act with a family member as custodian. Other alternatives include Section 529 plans and, of course, direct payments of tuition and medical expense by grandparents and other family members.

> Majority is determined by state law. Generally, the age of majority is 18.

Your wealth transfer team can help you with the mechanics, which can be tricky. For example, if grandmother transfers funds to a custodial account – and names herself as custodian – she will be treated as the owner of the account for estate tax purposes. Another issue: transfers to trusts do not always qualify for the annual gift tax exclusion. For this reason, you may need to use vehicles like "Crummey trusts" or "2503(c) trusts," which can qualify as annual exclusion gifts.

> Some trusts give beneficiaries "Crummey powers," i.e., a right to withdraw periodic contributions made by the grantor. The purpose of a Crummey power (which is generally not exercised) is to qualify part or all of the grantor's transfers for the gift tax annual exclusion (see Chapter Five).

Throughout, be sure to think carefully about issues of control. One drawback to Uniform Transfers to Minors Accounts is that control of the gifted funds passes to the child when she turns 18 or 21. In contrast, a trust does not necessarily terminate with full withdrawal at majority.

### 4. Why might I want to use a trust to transfer wealth to my minor children at my death?

A trust is generally the best alternative for a minor child's inheritance. Unlike a guardianship, which will require continued monitoring by a guardianship judge and will terminate when the child attains age 18 or 21, trusts are fully private and much more flexible – you decide the terms, including termination date and standards for distributions and withdrawals.

## 5. *Why might I consider making lifetime gifts to my adult children?*

Lifetime gifts to adult children give you, as the parent, the ability to "test drive" your wealth transfer plan. They can also give your children experience in managing significant amounts of money. Sometimes, however, lifetime gifts are driven by the circumstances of a child's life, such as divorce, illness or unemployment. If this is your situation, you will want to consider the impact of these "ad hoc" transfers on your overall wealth transfer plan. If you make unequal gifts to children, you should consider whether or not they should be equalized, either during your life or at your death. In any event, you should explain your intentions carefully and tactfully. With good communication, children are more apt to feel that they were treated fairly.

## 6. *Why might I want to use a trust to transfer wealth to an adult child?*

Much depends on the amount of money in question, the age (or financial maturity) of the child and whether the trust will continue after the child's lifetime. Smaller transfers are usually made outright while larger transfers may be made in trust. A trust is also more frequently used for children without a proven ability to handle finances. The child may serve as co-trustee together with an institutional or bank trustee whom the child can replace under specified circumstances. Trusts are often used to protect a child's inheritance in the event of a divorce or a claim by a creditor.

As the potential grantors of their children's trusts, parents need to consider:

- How much trust income and/or principal should be distributed, and at what intervals;

- When and to whom the balance of the trust principal should be distributed after the child dies;

- What discretionary authority the trustee should have – no one can predict what a child will need or when; and

- The transfer tax advantages that a trust may provide.

In the end, the decision about how to leave children their inheritance comes down to values, to the meaning of money within the family and to the parents' judgment.

### 7. *How much control should I give my adult children over their trusts?*

One common pattern is to name children co-trustees of their trusts, with liberal powers of withdrawal and complete termination of the trust at a specified age. Another solution – often tax driven – is making the child a life beneficiary, with the remainder passing to future generations. (A generation-skipping dynasty trust is one example.) Some parents combine a life estate with a power of appointment, enabling the child, for example, to transfer trust property outright or in trust to other family members or to charity.

If you are uncomfortable with giving a child authority to withdraw trust assets, discuss alternatives with your wealth transfer team. For example, consider giving a trustee broad discretionary powers. Under a broad distribution standard, the trustee can determine how much or how little to distribute. In other situations, you might want to incorporate a narrow standard into the document, allowing distributions only for education or health or basic support. See also the description of spendthrift trusts in Chapter Eight.

**8.  *How can I provide financial security for a disabled child?***

A *special needs trust* (or *supplemental needs trust*) can help you provide for the needs of a disabled individual without interfering with eligibility for government benefits.

The trustee of the special needs trust is authorized to provide for the child's welfare, but only to the extent that such support is not provided by the government. The trustee can directly pay medical costs, rent, tuition, transportation or basic maintenance expenses, but is precluded from making direct payment to the child.

If the trust is intended to supplement, rather than replace, government benefits, it must be properly drafted. It is important to select qualified professionals with expertise in this particular area and in the laws of the state where the child resides.

**9.  *When should I introduce children to their trustee?***

It is important for your children to know all the members of the wealth transfer team with whom they will work at your death or disability. This should include your accountant, your executor, your trustee and your financial advisor.

In particular, children who will one day be trust beneficiaries need to develop a good relationship with their trustee. This is especially important when the trustee will have discretionary authority to make or withhold distributions. It is critical for the trustee to know as much as possible about the children – and for the children to feel comfortable with the trustee.

# CHAPTER THIRTEEN

# Transfers to Grandchildren, Grandnephews and Grandnieces

*Family dynamics and taxes, in particular the generation-skipping transfer tax, are prime issues to keep in mind when considering transfers to grandchildren, grandnephews and grandnieces.*

1. *What special issues should I consider when planning transfers to grandchildren, grandnephews and grandnieces?*
When grandparents have more wealth than their children reasonably need, transfers to grandchildren make a great deal of sense. Generally, the same concerns arise as with transfers to children:

- Should you equalize transfers?
- How much is enough?
- Should the transfer be outright or in trust?
- How can you make the transfer tax-efficient?

In addition, you should remember to discuss your plans for your grandchildren with your children. Especially consider whether your gift will diminish the parents' control over your grandchild – young people who anticipate a large inheritance often gain a false sense of independence.

One solution is to leave the grandchild's inheritance in trust, with the parents serving as co-trustees with a bank trustee.

*Equalizing gifts*
Another sensitive issue is what to do if you have different numbers of grandchildren from each of your children. If you leave equal amounts to each child and an additional equal amount to each grandchild, will the child with fewer offspring view this as an unequal gift?

The structure of the annual gift tax exclusion favors equal gifts to family members during life. Parents who leave their estates to, or in trust for, children generally leave equal amounts to each child, regardless of the number of grandchildren in each branch. Likewise, parents who include grandchildren in their wealth transfer plans usually leave equal amounts to each grandchild. There is no right or wrong answer to this issue, but you should discuss the choice you make with your family so that they understand your intentions.

### 2. When do I need to worry about the generation-skipping transfer tax?

The generation-skipping transfer tax potentially applies not only to transfers to grandchildren, but in any situation where beneficiaries are more than one generation younger than the donor. Transfers to relatives such as grandnieces or grandnephews – or to friends more than 37½ years younger – all may trigger GST.

The good news is that the annual exclusion and exclusion for direct payment of tuition and medical expense can work for GST purposes as well as for gift tax purposes. The annual exclusion, in particular, will generally shelter smaller transfers – holiday gifts, a trip abroad – from GST.

*Note: The annual exclusion rules that apply to transfers in trust are different for GST purposes than for gift tax purposes.*

### 3. I plan to make significant generation-skipping transfers. How can I avoid the generation-skipping transfer tax?

Discuss any potential generation-skipping transfers with your wealth transfer team. The generation-skipping transfer tax is imposed *in addition* to the gift or estate tax. If the generation-skipping transfer tax applies, the total tax due is likely to be quite large and could significantly reduce the amount available to your beneficiaries.

> **Example:** Charles makes a lifetime gift of $5 million to his grandson Cole. Charles will pay gift tax on the transfer of $2,392,500 and, in addition, generation-skipping transfer tax of $1,350,000, for a combined tax of $3,742,500.

Your advisors will work to stretch your available GST exemption (see Appendix C) so that it covers any GST transfers that would otherwise be taxable. Often this is accomplished by the transfer of assets to generation-skipping trusts.

In some situations, a GST trust will provide for both children and grandchildren as beneficiaries, e.g., "income and discretionary principal to 'Child' for life, then outright to 'Grandchild.'" Alternately, if 'Child' is already well provided for, a separate GST trust may be established just for 'Grandchild.'

In situations where there is substantial wealth, a "dynasty trust" may be established to extend from generation to generation, perhaps in perpetuity. Although all states do not permit dynasty trusts, some states do. The laws of Delaware, for example, are very advantageous.

### THE VALUE OF A DYNASTY TRUST

If a GST trust distributes outright to your grandchildren, the assets will be taxed when they die. The dynasty trust solves this problem by allowing assets to escape several generations of taxation. You can create a dynasty trust during your lifetime or upon your death. Because your heirs do not have direct access to the trust assets, the trust is protected from estate taxes. The trust terms direct the trustee how to use trust principal and income for the benefit of beneficiaries within each generation.

# Preparing for Philanthropy

*Whether or not you think of yourself as a philanthropist, chances are you have made significant decisions about charitable transfers over the years. Chapter Fourteen shows how you can meld these choices into a coherent plan, one that may bring you and your family closer together. As always, taxes are an important consideration.*

## 1. What issues should I consider before making a charitable gift?

When you first consider a contribution to charity, ask yourself:

- What do you hope to accomplish through philanthropy?

- How does philanthropy fit into your overall financial and wealth transfer plans?

- How important is it to you that charitable giving creates a lasting family legacy?

- What type of charities do you want to benefit? Which specific charitable organizations best reflect your values and goals?

- How involved do you wish to be in the causes you hope to support?

- How will your family members be involved in the gifts?

- What legal structure(s) can you use for your charitable gifts (as an alternative to, or in addition to, making direct contributions) and what tax benefits would each provide?

Once you clarify your basic motivations and philanthropic interests, share your thoughts with your advisors so they can integrate your philanthropic objectives into your wealth transfer plan.

## 2. What is a "family charitable mission statement" and how can it facilitate philanthropy?

A family charitable mission statement facilitates the development of a comprehensive, coordinated and focused charitable giving plan. It translates your charitable giving philosophy into actionable and achievable objectives and procedures, which can guide you and your family for generations. Equally important, working together to create a family charitable mission statement is an excellent way to involve the entire family in the philanthropic process.

Your mission statement can specify what portion of the family wealth you wish to devote to philanthropic goals. It can also be very specific as to which causes and charities are to be supported, how and when donations will be made, and the criteria to use in evaluating whether to make further contributions.

**3.** *How do I develop my philanthropic plan?*

Defining your philanthropic goals and articulating a family charitable mission statement for your charitable giving activities are the first critical steps in developing a philanthropic plan. With an understanding of what you hope to accomplish, you can then explore various giving options with your advisors.

You and your wealth transfer team will determine which structures to use, such as trusts or donor advised funds, how to time your gifts to maximize the tax benefits and which assets to use to fund your charitable gift. You may even decide to adopt several charitable giving solutions in order to leverage your resources and provide opportunities for your family to participate in your philanthropic activities.

Just as key life events should trigger a review of your wealth transfer plan, changes in your financial or personal situation should prompt a review of your philanthropic plan.

**4. *How important are tax rules when making charitable gifting?***

In addition to determining the size of your charitable deduction, tax rules will likely influence the timing and structure of your gift. For example, your accountant may suggest that you time your contributions to offset a surge of taxable income from a bonus or sale. Similarly, your estate planning attorney may advise that certain types of structures will not qualify for the charitable deduction – whereas others (such as charitable gift annuities or charitable remainder trusts) will enable you to provide for family members as well as charity.

Before making a substantial charitable gift, consult with your wealth transfer team and the planned giving officer from the recipient charity. A carefully structured transfer can generate a significant charitable deduction; a transfer that ignores the tax rules will not.

**5. *How can I be sure my charitable transfers qualify for the charitable deduction?***

For the reasons explained above, you should review significant transfers with your wealth transfer team. In general, the more you know about a potential charity – mission statement, annual report, tax returns – the more beneficial the discussion will be. A great deal of information is available online, either at the charity's website or at sources such as GuideStar, Charity Navigator or the Better Business Bureau Wise Giving Alliance.

The most basic requirement is that the recipient be tax-exempt. Most tax-exempt charities are publicly supported organizations, e.g., United Way, YMCA, American Red Cross, the Girl Scouts, churches and nonprofit schools. To determine if a charity is tax-exempt, check the IRS list of qualified charities at *www.irs.gov/charities* or a convenient online service such as GuideStar (*www.GuideStar.org*).

SITUATION: WIDOW IN HER 70s.
Jane is a widow in her 70s, living in Naples, Florida. The only living member of her family is her daughter Susan (age 50), a renowned paleontologist who travels widely and visits Naples once a year. Susan has a modest salary and no retirement savings.

Jane's assets, including her home and investment portfolio, exceed $10 million. All of her assets are held in her revocable trust with Jane and a corporate fiduciary as co-trustees.

Jane's estate plan was last revised in 1990, immediately after her husband's death. It provides for distribution of the entire estate outright to Susan. Susan is also named as agent under Jane's powers of attorney for property and health care.

SOLUTION
If Jane were to die in 2008, the estate tax on transfer of $10 million to Susan would be $3.6 million ($10 million – $2 million available estate tax exemption x 45%). Susan would receive $6.4 million.

After reading *Legacy*, Jane considers her goals and sets up a meeting with her estate planning attorney and her accountant. She tells them that her objectives are to:

- Revise her powers of attorney;

- Provide Susan with income in her retirement;

- Set up a scholarship fund in paleontology at Susan's university; and

- Minimize the estate tax due on her own death.

She asks if one or more charitable trusts might help her achieve her objectives. Her estate planner proposes the following:

*During Jane's lifetime*
Jane updates her powers of attorney for property and health care, naming a close friend who lives nearby as her agent.

Jane transfers $3 million immediately to an irrevocable charitable trust (a charitable lead trust) that:

- Makes payments ($175,000 annually) for 15 years to endow the scholarship fund; and

- Distributes outright to Susan at the end of the 15-year term (when Susan is 65), providing funds for Susan's retirement. Assuming a steady 6% annual rate of return on the trust's investments, Susan would receive about $3 million.

*At Jane's death*
Jane's plan transfers $7 million to an irrevocable charitable trust (a charitable remainder trust) that:

- Makes payments to Susan for life (initial annual payment will be $350,000); and

- Distributes to the scholarship fund at Susan's death.

Jane implements the proposed plan. She is content because she has provided generously for Susan, left herself with sufficient funds for her own lifetime and reduced her potential estate tax by more than $1.6 million. Jane's updated powers of attorney for health care and property help ensure that her needs will be attended to even if Susan is unavailable.

# Making
# Charitable Gifts

*Chapter Fifteen is all about choosing charitable strategies that work for you. We discuss a variety of alternatives, from outright gifts to donor advised funds and private foundations.*

## 1. How do I decide which assets to give to charity?

The most common funding sources for philanthropy are cash, publicly traded stock or a combination of both. Some donors may have a broader range of assets to choose from however, such as closely held stock or retirement plans.

From a tax standpoint, it's generally preferable to sell a *depreciated* asset, take the tax loss and donate the cash proceeds. On the other hand, donating a long-term *appreciated* asset generally means avoiding or deferring capital gains tax on the sale – while at the same time garnering an income tax charitable deduction.

In some situations, special tax rules will become important – for example, for fractional gifts of art or for lifetime transfers of intellectual property. Your wealth transfer team can sort through the alternatives with you, working to find the right charitable vehicle for each type of asset. You may be surprised at the range of opportunities.

## 2. I have read that there are many ways to give to charity. What are some common alternatives?

The most common choices include:

- Outright gifts;
- Donor advised funds;
- Charitable gift annuities;
- Charitable remainder trusts; and
- Private foundations.

Many factors are involved in choosing the most appropriate solution – including your motivations, objectives and financial situation. The size of the gift does not necessarily determine the choice of charitable vehicle.

### 3. *What is a donor advised fund and how can it help me achieve my objectives?*

A donor advised fund is a separate account for which you, as donor, and your designees (as advisors) have the power to recommend grants and investments. The account is owned and held by a sponsoring charity, which may or may not receive a certain percentage of grants made. Often, the sponsoring charity is a community foundation. Less frequently, it is a large public charity, such as a hospital or educational institution. Major financial institutions also offer associated donor advised funds.

Donor advised funds have become increasingly popular because of their versatility and ease of operation. All of the administrative details are handled by the sponsoring charity. The sponsoring charity will also make sure your designated charity is tax-exempt and, in some cases, will offer assistance in making grant recommendations.

A transfer to a donor advised fund may be made during life or at death and is treated for tax purposes as a direct transfer to the sponsoring public charity. Therefore, the applicable income tax limitations are those for gifts to public charities:

- Annual deductions for gifts of cash are limited to 50% of adjusted gross income; and

- Annual deductions for gifts of securities are limited to 30% of adjusted gross income.

The gift or estate tax charitable deduction will equal the fair market value of the cash and property transferred.

**4.  *What is a charitable gift annuity?***

A charitable gift annuity is a type of sale: you transfer assets to the charity (typically a larger nonprofit organization) in exchange for annual income – usually a fixed percentage of your gift. The annuity may be paid to you and/or a third party – a spouse, partner, child or friend.

For income tax purposes, your charitable deduction is based on the excess of your contribution over the cost of a comparable commercial annuity. If you transfer appreciated assets for the annuity, the annuity beneficiaries will recognize capital gains as they receive their payments. You may want to compare the advantages and disadvantages of a gift annuity with those of a charitable remainder trust.

**5.  *How do charitable transfers to trusts work? In particular, what are the advantages of a charitable remainder trust?***

Some charitable trusts benefit one or more charities; others benefit both individuals and charities. This flexibility can be very useful when addressing a wide range of family situations.

One popular choice is the charitable remainder unitrust, where payments are made to individuals (e.g., you, your partner or a child) over time, with the charity receiving the remainder at the end of the trust term. There are four varieties of unitrusts, including the flip unitrust, which is well suited to transfers of illiquid assets, such as closely held stock or real estate.

Ordinarily, people fund these trusts with appreciated assets (e.g., securities, debt-free real estate or collectibles) because they want to defer the capital gains tax that would otherwise be due on the asset's sale. With a charitable remainder trust, tax is paid only as payments from the trust are received. For a similar reason, an IRA is also an ideal funding choice: the charitable remainder trust spreads out income tax liability for your beneficiaries, while reducing your taxable estate by the value of the remainder gift to charity.

**6.  *What is a charitable lead trust and when should it be considered?***

Charitable lead trusts (CLT) make sense if you want to minimize estate and generation-skipping tax by delaying the transfer of wealth to the next generations. The charitable lead trust makes payments to charity for an initial term. At the end of the term, the remaining principal is distributed to the individual beneficiaries, often the donor's children or grandchildren. A CLT can be either testamentary (created by your will or trust) or inter vivos (created during your lifetime).

Because the gift to individuals is deferred, the donor leverages her estate, gift or generation-skipping tax exemption to the fullest. The key here is the time value of money: a gift of a future interest (the remainder) has less value than a gift of a present interest. As a result, the amount of gift, estate or generation-skipping tax exemption needed to protect the remainder from tax is minimized.

The charitable lead annuity trust (CLAT) works best for deferred transfers to children while the charitable lead unitrust (CLUT) works best for generation-skipping transfers.

**Example:** Marilyn, age 60, is active in her community and makes significant transfers to charity each year. Her net worth totals $20 million. At her death, she plans to leave $10 million of her estate to her daughter Sara, with the rest, after payment of taxes, to charity. Marilyn dies suddenly in December of 2008 without having considered using a charitable lead trust in her plan. Based on these assumptions:

- Sara receives $10 million at Marilyn's death;
- Marilyn's estate pays $6.545 million of federal estate tax on the $10 million transfer to Sara; and
- Charity receives $3.455 million at Marilyn's death.

**Alternative:** Same facts as above except that, after talking with her advisors, Marilyn decides to create a $5 million charitable lead annuity trust, with Sara as the remainder beneficiary. The trust, which Marilyn funds in March of 2008, pays an annual annuity of $250,000 to a new private foundation for 20 years. At the end of the 20 years, the trust will distribute to Sara.

In addition, Marilyn and her advisors provide for a $5 million outright transfer to Sara, to occur at Marilyn's death. The rest of the estate, after payment of taxes, will go to charity.

Based on these assumptions and an expected annual growth rate of 7% on the trust assets:

- Sara receives $13.4 million, $5 million at Marilyn's death and $8.4 million in 2028, when the charitable trust terminates;
- Marilyn's estate pays $3.664 million on the $13.4 million transfer (federal gift tax of $200,895 and federal estate tax of $3,463,598); and
- Charity receives $11.536 million, $6.536 million at Marilyn's death and $5 million over the term of the charitable lead trust.

Tax outcome: Taxes are reduced by almost $3 million.

### 7. *What is the role of private foundations in charitable gifting?*

There are more than 70,000 grant-making private foundations in the United States. Unlike public charities, private foundations are supported not by the general public but by a very limited number of donors – typically a corporation or a high-net-worth family. More than half of all private foundations are family foundations, controlled by individual donors and their descendants, advisors and friends.

The income tax charitable deduction for lifetime transfers to private foundations is limited by the "percentage of adjusted gross income" rules. Gifts of cash are subject to a 30% limitation; gifts of publicly traded stock are subject to a 20% limitation. Importantly, the income tax charitable deduction for transfers to a private foundation of long-term appreciated assets other than publicly traded stock (such as real estate or closely held stock) is generally limited to the donor's cost. For this reason, most lifetime transfers to private foundations are funded with cash or publicly traded stock.

> **PROMOTING FAMILY PHILANTHROPY**
>
> Families who create a private foundation usually do so to promote family unity and a tradition of giving. Sometimes, however, family discord can arise if family members support widely disparate charitable endeavors. To minimize conflict, some families choose to set up individual foundations for each of their children, allowing each child to make grants as he pleases from his foundation.

In contrast, if a transfer to a private foundation is made at death, the unlimited estate tax charitable deduction is available, whether the asset being transferred is cash, publicly traded securities, real estate or closely held stock.

Although private foundations are exempt from income tax, most pay a 2% excise tax on their net investment income, including capital gains. Private foundations are also subject to a variety of penalty taxes designed to ensure that donors do not benefit, directly or indirectly, from the foundation's assets and income. One downside of a private foundation is its administrative complexity. For example, the tax rules require annual distributions equal to at least 5% of average monthly asset value, with a 30% penalty tax on late payments. There are also complex rules on self-dealing, excess business holdings, jeopardizing investments and excess expenditures, all with associated penalty excise taxes.

To keep their foundations legally compliant, donors typically turn to their accountants or a financial services provider who will serve as agent or trustee.

# PART SIX

# TAKING YOUR NEXT STEP

# Summarizing
# Key Points

*In the final section, we summarize the key points of the previous chapters, focusing on specific actions you can take to create and implement a wealth transfer plan that will meet your objectives today as well as in the future.*

### Getting started

Throughout *Legacy*, we have discussed how a wealth transfer plan should reflect not only your financial objectives, but also your values and beliefs. Integrating your various goals into a cohesive plan – and sharing that plan with your family – contributes to the creation of your legacy.

After you have examined your needs and goals, you will need to assemble your advisory team. Depending on your situation, your team may include family members as well as professional advisors such as your estate planning attorney, accountant and financial advisor. We recommend that you prepare for your meeting with your advisors by preparing an inventory of your assets. To help you in this effort, we have provided a sample inventory form as Appendix B.

### Developing and implementing your plan

Working with your team, you will create a comprehensive wealth transfer plan that 1) expresses your financial objectives, personal values and beliefs, and philanthropic goals, and 2) specifies how you want your wealth transferred during your life and at your death to achieve them. Your wealth transfer documents will likely include:

- Powers of attorney;
- A will; and
- Revocable and irrevocable trusts.

In order for your plan to accomplish its intended objectives, you will need to:

- Share your documents with the appropriate individuals and institutions, such as family members, trustees and executors;

- Update beneficiary designations on retirement plans and insurance policies; and

- Fund your trusts by transferring assets to them.

### Updating and revising

If your goals and needs change as a result of a significant life event, you will want to revisit your plan with your family and team members to ensure that it continues to accomplish your objectives. At a minimum, your plan should be reviewed by your estate planning attorney every five years to incorporate changes in applicable state and federal law.

### In conclusion

In our experience, the best wealth transfer plans build on life-long values, using tax and financial expertise to achieve carefully considered personal objectives.

We welcome the opportunity to discuss your situation and illustrate how we can work with you and your professional advisors to help develop and implement a wealth transfer plan that preserves what it may have taken you a lifetime to build.

# FINANCIAL INFORMATION TO ASSEMBLE

The guidelines below can serve as a frame of reference as you assemble the information your advisors will need. Of course, as you proceed you'll probably find it necessary to supply additional information pertinent to your particular situation.

- List all assets and liabilities accurately. Include regular payment dates and amounts due (see Appendix B).

- Provide complete information about assets other than cash or securities (real estate, automobiles and boats are examples). Indicate whether these assets are in your name only or if they are owned jointly with your spouse or another individual. Also, be sure to include the location – especially if it's out of state – of each asset.

- Indicate names, ages and addresses of family members or friends you intend to name as beneficiaries.

- A copy of your current will, trust(s) and powers of attorney.

- Include explanations, current balances and projections (if available) of all employee benefit plan entitlements, such as 401(k) plans and individual retirement accounts, as well as the beneficiary designations of the plans.

- Supply copies of any gift tax returns previously filed.

- Provide copies of any important documents, particularly those relating to divorce, annulment, separation or adoption. Don't overlook deeds of ownership for real estate.

- If you are married, outline how you want your property to pass in the following situations:

  — You predecease your spouse;

  — Your spouse predeceases you;

  — One or more of your children predecease you; or

  — You predecease a parent or other older relative who may not remain financially independent.

- Consider how you would respond to the following questions.

  — In the event you and your spouse die at the same time (in a common accident, for example), at what ages would you want property to be available to your children without restriction?

  — At this time, should the need arise, whom would you wish to be designated as guardians of your children? If your chosen guardian(s) become unable to care for your children, whom would you want to succeed them?

- Names, addresses and contacts at all charitable organizations (including schools and universities) you expect to mention in your estate plan and the type or amount of property you intend them to receive. Note whether or not you already have indicated your intentions to the planned recipient.

- Specifically list items of personal property you want particular individuals to have upon your death if you predecease your spouse, and what other dispositions you would make if your spouse predeceases you.

■  Think about who you might appoint as executor and
   trustee. These are important decisions because the
   executor and trustee are responsible for managing and
   distributing your assets in the way you specify.

# PERSONAL INVENTORY

## BALANCE SHEET

| ASSETS | YOURS | YOUR SPOUSE'S | JOINT | TOTAL |
|---|---|---|---|---|
| Cash and Short–Term Investments (Schedule A) | | | | |
| Stocks and Bonds (Readily Marketable) (Schedule B) | | | | |
| Cash Value – Life Insurance (Schedule D) | | | | |
| Other Liquid Assets | | | | |
| TOTAL LIQUID ASSETS | | | | |
| Notes Receivable (Schedule C) | | | | |
| Accounts Receivable (Expected within 1 year) (Schedule C) | | | | |
| Real Estate Owned – Personal Use (Schedule E) | | | | |
| Vested Profit-Sharing Benefits/Deferred Compensation (Schedule F) | | | | |
| IRA/KEOGH Accounts | | | | |
| Stocks and Bonds (Not Readily Marketable) (Schedule G) | | | | |
| Business Interests (Equity) | | | | |
| Real Estate Owned – Investment Purposes (Schedule H) | | | | |
| General and/or Limited Partnership Interests (Schedule I) | | | | |
| Personal Property (including collections) | | | | |
| Other Assets | | | | |
| TOTAL ASSETS | | | | |
| **LIABILITIES** | **YOURS** | **YOUR SPOUSE'S** | **JOINT** | **TOTAL** |
| Notes Payable to Banks – Secured (Schedule J) | | | | |
| Notes Payable to Banks – Unsecured (Schedule J) | | | | |
| Notes Payable to Others (Schedule J) | | | | |
| Outstanding Credit Card Balances | | | | |
| Other Accounts Payable (Schedule J) | | | | |
| Amounts Owing to Brokers | | | | |
| Taxes and Interest Payable (Unpaid but Accrued) | | | | |
| Policy Loans (Life Insurance) (Schedule D) | | | | |
| Mortgages and Obligations on Real Estate Owned (Schedule E) | | | | |
| Mortgages and Obligations on Investment Real Estate Owned (Schedule H) | | | | |
| Other Liabilities | | | | |
| TOTAL LIABILITIES | | | | |
| Net Worth (Total Assets Minus Total Liabilities) | | | | |

## SCHEDULE A: CASH AND SHORT-TERM INVESTMENTS
*(Including Certificates of Deposit, Commercial Paper, Money Market Funds, Etc.)*

| NAME OF INSTITUTION | SAVINGS ACCOUNTS | CHECKING ACCOUNTS | OTHER SHORT-TERM INVESTMENTS | OWNER (YOU/YOUR SPOUSE/ JOINT) | TOTAL |
|---|---|---|---|---|---|
| | | | | | |
| | | | | | |
| | | | | | |
| | | | | | |
| | | | | | |
| | | | | | |
| | | | | | |
| | | | | | |
| | | | | | |
| | | | | | |

## SCHEDULE B: STOCKS, BONDS, GOVERNMENT SECURITIES

| NO. OF SHARES OR PAR VALUE OF BONDS | DESCRIPTION | RESTRICTED | PLEDGED | OWNER (YOU/YOUR SPOUSE/ JOINT) | LISTED/ UNLISTED | COST | MARKET VALUE |
|---|---|---|---|---|---|---|---|
| | | ❑ | ❑ | | | | |
| | | ❑ | ❑ | | | | |
| | | ❑ | ❑ | | | | |
| | | ❑ | ❑ | | | | |
| | | ❑ | ❑ | | | | |
| | | ❑ | ❑ | | | | |
| | | ❑ | ❑ | | | | |
| | | ❑ | ❑ | | | | |
| | | ❑ | ❑ | | | | |
| | | ❑ | ❑ | | | | |

## SCHEDULE C: NOTES AND ACCOUNTS RECEIVABLE

| FROM WHOM | ORIGINAL AMOUNT | MONTHLY PAYMENTS | MATURITY DATES | INTEREST RATES | DESCRIPTION OF COLLATERAL | PLEDGED | BALANCE DUE |
|---|---|---|---|---|---|---|---|
| | | | | | | ❏ | |
| | | | | | | ❏ | |
| | | | | | | ❏ | |
| | | | | | | ❏ | |
| | | | | | | ❏ | |
| | | | | | | ❏ | |
| | | | | | | ❏ | |
| | | | | | | ❏ | |
| | | | | | | ❏ | |
| | | | | | | ❏ | |

## SCHEDULE D: INSURANCE – LIFE (GROUP/WHOLE) AND DISABILITY

| GROUP/WHOLE LIFE AMOUNTS | NAME OF COMPANY | BENEFICIARIES | OWNER (YOU/YOUR SPOUSE/ JOINT) | POLICY LOANS OUTSTANDING | GROSS CASH VALUE |
|---|---|---|---|---|---|
| | | | | | |
| | | | | | |
| | | | | | |
| TERM POLICIES | | | | | |
| | | | | | |
| | | | | | |
| | | | | | |
| DISABILITY POLICIES | | | | | |
| | | | | | |
| | | | | | |
| | | | | | |

## SCHEDULE E: REAL ESTATE OWNED – PERSONAL USE

| ADDRESS OF PROPERTY AND NAME OF MORTGAGE HOLDER | TITLE IN NAME OF | DATE PURCHASED | COST | AMOUNT OWED | MORTGAGE MATURITY | MARKET VALUE |
|---|---|---|---|---|---|---|
| | | | | | | |
| | | | | | | |
| | | | | | | |
| | | | | | | |
| | | | | | | |

## SCHEDULE F: VESTED INTEREST IN DEFERRED COMPENSATION/ PROFIT-SHARING PLANS

| COMPANY NAME | % VESTED | OWNER (YOU/YOUR SPOUSE) | MANNER OF PAYOUT (ANNUITY, LUMP SUM, ETC) | DISTRIBUTION DATE | BENEFICIARY | AMOUNT |
|---|---|---|---|---|---|---|
| | | | | | | |
| | | | | | | |
| | | | | | | |
| | | | | | | |
| | | | | | | |

## SCHEDULE G: STOCKS AND BONDS (NOT READILY MARKETABLE)

| DESCRIPTION OF SECURITIES | OWNER (YOU/YOUR SPOUSE/JOINT) | NO. OF SHARES OWNED | % OWNERSHIP | PLEDGED | BOOK VALUE | |
|---|---|---|---|---|---|---|
| | | | | | AS OF DATE | AMOUNT |
| | | | | ❏ | | |
| | | | | ❏ | | |
| | | | | ❏ | | |
| | | | | ❏ | | |
| | | | | ❏ | | |

## SCHEDULE H: REAL ESTATE OWNED – INVESTMENT PURPOSES

| A. OWNER B. PURCHASE DATE C. COST | ADDRESS OF PROPERTY AND LENDER INFORMATION | TYPE OF PROPERTY | % OWNED | PRESENT MARKET VALUE | AMOUNT OF MORTGAGE & LIENS | GROSS RENTAL INCOME | MORTGAGE PAYMENTS, TAXES, & MISC | NET RENTAL INCOME |
|---|---|---|---|---|---|---|---|---|
| A.<br><br>B.<br><br>C. | Address of Property<br><br>Lender's name/ address | | | | | | | |
| A.<br><br>B.<br><br>C. | Address of Property<br><br>Lender's name/ address | | | | | | | |
| A.<br><br>B.<br><br>C. | Address of Property<br><br>Lender's name/ address | | | | | | | |

## SCHEDULE I: GENERAL AND/OR LIMITED PARTNERSHIP INTEREST

| NAME OF PARTNERSHIP | TYPE OF INVESTMENT | LIMITED OR GENERAL | AMOUNT INVESTED | FAIR MARKET VALUE OF PARTNERSHIP INTEREST |
|---|---|---|---|---|
| | | | | |
| | | | | |
| | | | | |
| | | | | |
| | | | | |

## SCHEDULE J: NOTES AND ACCOUNTS PAYABLE

| TO WHOM | ORIGINAL AMOUNT AND DATE | MONTHLY PAYMENT | MATURITY DATE | INTEREST RATE | DESCRIPTION OF COLLATERAL (IF ANY) | BALANCE OWING |
|---|---|---|---|---|---|---|
|  |  |  |  |  |  |  |
|  |  |  |  |  |  |  |
|  |  |  |  |  |  |  |
|  |  |  |  |  |  |  |
|  |  |  |  |  |  |  |

## ADDITIONAL INFORMATION:
## UNEXERCISED COMPANY STOCK OPTIONS

| NAME OF COMPANY | EXPIRATION DATE | NO. OF SHARES | TOTAL MARKET VALUE | TOTAL EXERCISE (NO. SHARES X EXERCISE PRICE) | NET PROCEEDS (TOTAL MARKET VALUE – TOTAL EXERCISE) |
|---|---|---|---|---|---|
|  |  |  |  |  |  |
|  |  |  |  |  |  |
|  |  |  |  |  |  |
|  |  |  |  |  |  |
|  |  |  |  |  |  |

# 2008
# TAX TABLES

## THE INCOME TAX - 2008

### Regular Income Tax

| Married Filing Jointly | | Single | |
| --- | --- | --- | --- |
| Taxable Income | Rate | Taxable Income | Rate |
| $65,101 – $131,450 | 25% | $32,551 – $78,850 | 25% |
| $131,451 – $200,300 | 28% | $78,851 – $164,550 | 28% |
| $200,301 – $357,700 | 33% | $164,551 – $357,700 | 33% |
| Over $357,700 | 35% | Over $357,700 | 35% |

*Note: Lower rates for lower income taxpayers: 10% and 15%*

### Qualified Dividends & Long-Term Capital Gains

| Married Filing Jointly | | Single | |
| --- | --- | --- | --- |
| Taxable Income | Rate | Taxable Income | Rate |
| $65,101 and up | 15% | $32,551 and up | 15% |

*Note: Lower rate for lower income taxpayers: 0%*

# THE GIFT TAX - 2008

| Aggregate Lifetime Transfers | Rate |
|---|---|
| Over $1 million – $1.25 million | 41% |
| Over $1.25 million – $1.5 million | 43% |
| Over $1.5 million – $2 million | 45% |
| Over $2 million | 45% |

Notes:
- *$1 million lifetime exemption per donor*
- *$12,000 annual exclusion*
- *Unlimited exclusion for direct payments of tuition and medical expense*
- *Unlimited marital deduction*
- *Unlimited charitable deduction*

## THE ESTATE TAX - 2008

| Aggregate Transfers During Life and at Death | Rate |
|---|---|
| Over $2 million | 45% |

*Notes:*
- *$2 million exemption per decedent*
- *Unlimited marital deduction*
- *Unlimited charitable deduction*

## THE GENERATION-SKIPPING TAX - 2008

| Aggregate Generation-Skipping Transfers During Life and at Death | Rate |
|---|---|
| Over $2 million | 45% |

*Notes:*
- *$2 million exemption per transferor*
- *$12,000 annual exclusion*
- *Unlimited exclusion for direct payments of tuition and medical expense*

# Glossary of Terms

**Agent**
A person who acts on behalf of another person at that person's request. The agent controls the property but does not have ownership.

**Annual Exclusion, or Gift Tax Annual Exclusion**
The amount of money or property (in 2008, $12,000 for an individual and $24,000 for a married couple) that may be given as a gift to a recipient each year without incurring a gift tax.

**Beneficiary**
An individual named as the recipient of the income or principal of an estate or trust.

**Bequest**
A gift of personal property or a specific cash amount, initiated by a will; a legacy.

## Community Property
Property in which a husband and wife each have one-half interest by reason of their marital status. (Not all states have community property.)

## Contest of a Will
Legal proceedings to prevent or alter distribution of estate assets as described in a will.

## Domicile
Your permanent home; the place where you intend to return after temporary absences.

## Estate Planning (or Wealth Transfer Planning)
The process of identifying your assets, determining how you would like them distributed, and using all resources available to minimize the effect of transfer taxes. Three key elements make up a wealth transfer plan – a will, trust(s) and durable power of attorney.

## Executor
The individual or institution named in a will and charged with carrying out the provisions it specifies. A co-executor serves as executor sharing duties with one or more designated institutions or individuals. Sometimes referred to as a Personal Representative.

## Fiduciary
An individual or institution responsible for acting in the best interests of another party. A fiduciary is bound by law and duty to put aside personal interests and act in good faith when making decisions for the benefit of another.

## Funded Trust
A trust in which there has been a legal transfer of title to the trustee. This usually can be accomplished with relatively simple paperwork.

## Generation-Skipping Tax
A tax imposed on any generation-skipping transfer. The tax is intended to recover the amount equal to the transfer tax that would have been payable if the property were transferred outright to a child and then a grandchild.

**Grantor**
The person who creates a trust.

**Guardian**
An individual or institution named by a court to manage the property of a person who is judged incapable of handling his or her own affairs.

**Intestate**
Dying without a will.

**Irrevocable Trust**
A type of trust that cannot be altered or amended once established.

**Living Will**
A legal document in which an individual states, in advance of final illness or injury, his or her wishes regarding procedures and equipment designed to extend life.

**Power of Appointment**
The power given by an individual to another in a will or trust document to determine which persons will receive an interest in his or her estate. A general power of appointment may give the holder the right to distribute the trust's property to anyone, including himself or his estate. A special (or limited) power of appointment gives the holder the right to distribute the property among a limited group of people (such as descendants) or charities.

**Power of Attorney**
A legal document authorizing one individual to act as the agent or "attorney" for another (the principal). If the attorney is authorized to act on behalf of another for all matters, he or she has general power of attorney. Authority to act solely regarding specified situations is special power of attorney. If the authority granted extends beyond the disability of the principal, the attorney has durable power of attorney.

**Principal**
(1) One who employs an agent to act on his or her behalf. (2) One who is primarily liable on obligation. (3) The property of an estate other than the income from the property; the same as capital.

**Probate**
The public legal process whereby the legitimacy of a will is established and the administration of the estate is overseen by the court.

**Remainderman**
In the case of a trust, this term refers to the person or charity who will receive the principal of a trust when final distribution takes place.

**Revocable Trust**
A trust that can be altered or changed by the grantor during his or her lifetime. Afterwards, the trust becomes irrevocable and its assets are distributed according to its provisions. A revocable trust is sometimes called a living trust.

**Successor Trustee**
An individual or corporation designated to assume the role of trustee or co-trustee under certain circumstances, usually upon the death, resignation or incapacity of the initial trustee or co-trustee.

**Testamentary Trust**
A trust established by the terms of a will. The trust becomes effective and is fully funded only after the administration and settlement of an estate. Also called a trust under will.

**Title**
Legal ownership of property.

**Trust**
A legal, fiduciary relationship in which an individual or institution (the trustee) holds legal title to property with the responsibility for keeping or managing this property for the benefit of another person (the beneficiary).

**Trust Agreement**
A legal document that establishes a trust and outlines the rules and guidelines affecting its management and disposition.

**Trustee**
An individual or corporation empowered by law to hold legal title to property for the benefit of someone else. A co-trustee is an individual or institution who shares the fiduciary responsibilities of administering a trust.

**Vested Interest**
An interest that is certain to occur, as opposed to being contingent on an event that might not occur.

**Will**
A legal document in which a person states binding directions about what he or she wants done with his or her property after death.

# Index